TO MY DEAR WIFE,

WHO, LIKE HER SAINTED MOTHER, IS THE EMBODIMENT OF GENUINE MODESTY AND INTELLIGENT PIETY, THIS LITTLE VOLUME IS AFFECTIONATELY INSCRIBED.

ULYSSES S. GRANT

CONVERSATIONS

AND

UNPUBLISHED LETTERS

BY

M. J. CRAMER, D.D., LL.D.

EX-UNITED STATES MINISTER TO DENMARK AND TO SWITZERLAND

NEW YORK: EATON & MAINS

CINCINNATI: CURTS & JENNINGS

EATON & MAINS PRESS,
150 Fifth Avenue, New York.

PREFACE.

HAVING married, on the 27th of October, 1863, Miss Mary Frances Grant, youngest daughter of Mr. Jesse Root and Hannah Grant, of Covington, Ky., in the course of time I came thus into frequent contact with General Grant by visits at his home and otherwise. From the 6th to the 12th of July, 1878, General and Mrs. Grant were our guests at Copenhagen, Denmark.

During these visits, etc., the general and I conversed freely on various subjects; he readily answered all questions I put to him. I generally made a memorandum of the most interesting things he had said. He was one of the most instructive and interesting talkers I ever conversed with. His conversations had wit and humor in them. He was well versed, not only in the history of the United States, but also in regard to the various resources of the several States and Territories of the Union; to say nothing of his accurate knowledge of recent events in European and oriental countries.

We also exchanged letters. Some letters from him to other members of his father's family also fell into my hands. Some of them throw fresh light on both his private and public character, as well as on several of his earlier campaigns.

Neither the conversations nor the letters contained in the following pages have ever been published. Friends in civil and military life have heard me relate some of the former, and seen some of the latter; at their earnest solicitations I have consented to publish them all; otherwise it would never have occurred to me to do so.

I have endeavored to give the letters and the conversations in their historical order. Some of his earlier letters suggested questions which I put to him in order to elicit a fuller account of things alluded to therein.

My sole object in sending out this little volume is to serve the cause of truth in reference to a man who has played an important part in the recent history of our country.

M. J. C.

EAST ORANGE, N, J,, November, 1896.

TABLE OF CONTENTS.

ULYSSES S. GRANT.

CHAPTER I.

General Grant's Visit to Copenhagen — Ineidents and Views.

DURING his trip around the world General Grant visited Denmark. On July 5, 1878, they (the general and his wife) left Hamburg by rail for Lubeck, in order to see that quaint old city. On the evening of the same day they took a steamer for Copenhagen, arriving there the following morning at seven o'clock.[1] The

[1] John Russell Young in his work, *Around the World with General Grant* (vol. i, p. 436), writes as follows: "We leave Hamburg on July 6, journey rapidly through Schleswig-Holstein and Denmark, and cross the Great Belt," etc. Mr. Young may have done so, for he did not accompany General and Mrs. Grant to Copenhagen; nor did he call either on them or on me during the time they were my guests.

steamer on which they had come was flying the American flag in his honor. Quite a number of people had gathered at the landing, though nothing had been said or published about the date of his coming. They cheered him lustily as he and Mrs. Grant stepped ashore. They were driven at once to my house, where they were my guests until July 12, when they took a steamer for Christiania, Norway.

During these six days I accompanied them to different points and places of interest in and around Copenhagen, including two picture galleries, the Royal Library, six different museums, thirteen scientific and thirty charitable institutions. I was somewhat surprised at the general's accurate knowledge of Danish history, and of the agricultural, industrial, commercial, and financial resources of that country. Nor was his knowledge defective about the educational institutions of

Denmark. He informed me that he had carefully read both the diplomatic correspondence and the consular reports as soon as they were published by the state department. He was highly pleased at the perfection of the Danish public-school system, believing it to be about equal to ours. He thought that the Prussian, the Danish, and the American public schools were the best in the world, and that the percentage of illiteracy in these three countries was smaller than that of any other country.

We made several excursions to different parts of the kingdom. He noticed that where it was possible every foot of ground was under cultivation, that the people appeared to be intelligent, and to live in comfortable circumstances. He was correct in believing that there was no abject poverty among the Danish people. In a letter written to me from Paris on December 10, 1878, referring to his visit to Denmark, he writes among other things as follows: [1]

"Since leaving Copenhagen Mrs. Grant and I have visited every capital in Europe not previously visited by us. I can say with good earnestness that no part of our journeyings gave us more pleasure than that through the Scandinavian countries; and no people have impressed me more favorably."

Among the places we visited was Elsinore (*Dan.* Helsingör), a seaport twenty-four miles north of Copenhagen, situated on the west shore of the Sound, and at its narrowest part three and a half miles west southwest of the town of Helsingborg, in Sweden. Here the "Sound dues" were formerly collected of all vessels that passed either way; but during the first part of the present century they were

---

[1] The letters quoted in these pages are in my possession, and, if necessary, open for inspection or comparison.

gradually abolished by treaty arrangements with the different maritime nations. Here also Shakespeare laid the scene of his "Hamlet," an historical blunder on the part of the great dramatist, as Jutland, and not Seeland, was Hamlet's country. Hamlet's (supposed) grave and the pond where Ophelia is said to have drowned herself were pointed out to the party. Mrs. Grant had a copy of Hamlet with her, and seemed to believe all the guide said to us respecting those places, while the general, with a twinkle in his eyes and a smile on his lips, said: "I think these stories and places are as mythical as is the story of Holger Danske" (who is said to have resided in the vaults of the Castle of Kronborg near by, and who never appeared above ground save when the country was in danger, in order to march at the head of the Danish Army). But he believed in the reality of Saxo Grammaticus, a famous Danish writer of the twelfth century, who was born in this town.

Arrangements having been made through the usual diplomatic channels to present General and Mrs. Grant to their majesties, the King and Queen of Denmark, we drove, on Wednesday, July 10, to Bernstorff Castle, one of the royal summer residences, ten miles from Copenhagen, where we arrived at five o'clock P. M., the appointed hour. The interview between General and Mrs. Grant and their Danish majesties lasted an hour, during which various subjects relating to the United States and Denmark were discussed. The latter were surprised at the general's accurate knowledge of Danish history, politics, resources, etc. Some flattering remarks were made by the king and queen in reference to the writer which need not be repeated here.

The interview was followed by a banquet given by their majesties in honor of

General and Mrs. Grant, at which were present, besides the hosts and guests of honor, the crown prince and crown princess, the queen's court ladies, the king's ministers and court officials, the general of the army and the admiral of the navy, and the writer. The conversation was general, almost all the guests speaking English. It was noticed that General Grant drank no wine, except a few drops of champagne when the king proposed his health. Here it may be stated that General Grant declined with sincere thanks a banquet that the Minister of Foreign Affairs intended to give in his honor; as, also, one that the writer had wished to give at Klampenborg, a seaside resort, ten miles from Copenhagen. He said that he was tired of being "banqueted;" that they had come here to rest for a week.

After dinner the queen requested the general to inscribe his name in an album containing the autographs of emperors and empresses, kings and queens, princes and princesses, etc. He was watched by all the guests. Afterward Admiral Irminger, the commander of the king's steam yacht, said to the writer, "The manner in which General Grant inscribed his name in the album stamps him a great man."

One evening we went to the Tivoli Garden, a place of innocent amusement which people of all classes and ranks frequent during the summer season. On account of its fine and extensive grounds, its tasteful buildings and beautiful flower beds, its two superior orchestras, its open pantomime theater, panoramas, physical and chemical experiments, gymnastic feats, festive fireworks, its excellent restaurant, and small admission fee, the Tivoli Garden of Copenhagen is unrivaled by any similar institution in Europe. General Grant was highly pleased with it; he thought it a fine thing for those who are unable to spend the summer season in the country or at a seaside resort. "All cities ought to have similar places," he said, "where the rich and the poor, the high and the low may meet on a footing of equality; where they may have æsthetic, instructive, and other innocent amusements; and where all behave themselves in a proper manner, as is the case in the Tivoli Garden of Copenhagen. It would keep the poor people from grumbling, as well as from revolutionary tendencies."

CHAPTER II.

Experiences Previous to the War.

DURING his stay in Copenhagen as my guest General Grant expressed himself freely on any subject that I happened to broach. I asked him about his residence and business in Saint Louis previous to the war. He said: "I settled there as real estate agent late in 1858 or early in 1859. At first I believed that it would bring me more than a support; but I was disappointed in my hopes, for that business was even then overdone in that city, at least a dozen new houses having started about the same time I began. I had to look out for something else to do." Referring to this matter in a letter to his father, dated Saint Louis, Mo., August 20, 1859, he writes:

"I do not want to fly from one thing to another; nor would I; but I am compelled to make a living from the start, for which I am willing to give all my time and all my energy."

His father advised him to apply for a (as he supposed) vacant professorship of mathematics in Washington University. In reference thereto the general wrote him in the same letter as follows:

"As to the professorship you spoke of, that was filled some time ago; and were it not, I would stand no earthly chance. Washington University, where the vacancy was to be filled, is one of the best endowed institutions in the United States, and all the professorships are sought after by persons whose early advantages were the same as mine, and who have been engaged in teaching all their mature years. Quimby, who was the best mathematician in my class, and who was for several years an assistant at West Point and for nine years a professor in an institution in New York, was an unsuccessful applicant. The appointment is given to the most distinguished man in his department in the country, and an author."

The general also told me that he had made application for the appointment of county engineer, but failed to secure it. In reference to this latter he wrote in the same letter as follows:

"I am not oversanguine of getting the appointment mentioned in my last letter. The Board of Commissioners who make the appointment are divided, three Free Soilers to two opposed; and although friends who are recommending me are the very best citizens of this place and members of all parties, I fear they will make strictly party nominations for all the offices under their control. . . . Since putting in my application for the appointment of county engineer I have learned that the place is not likely to be filled before February next. What I shall do will depend entirely upon what I can get to do."

After having settled in Saint Louis as real estate agent he wrote to his father in reference to this matter, in a letter dated Saint Louis, Mo., March 12, 1859, as follows:

"We are now living in the lower part of the city, fully two miles from my office. The house is a comfortable little one, just suited to my means. We have one spare room, and also a spare bed in the children's room, so that we can accommodate any of our friends that are likely to come to see us. I want two of the girls [meaning two of his sisters] or all of them [he had at that time three unmarried sisters] for that matter, to come and pay us a long visit soon."

In reference to the appointment of county engineer referred to he wrote to his father, in a letter dated September 23, 1859, as follows:

"I have waited for some time to write you the result of the action of the county commissioners upon the appointment of a county engineer. The question has at length been settled, and, I am sorry to say, adversely to me. The two Democratic commissioners voted for me and the Free Soilers against me. What I shall now go at I have not determined, but I hope something before a great while. Next month I will get possession of my new house, when my expenses will be reduced so much that a very moderate salary will support me. . . . You may judge from the result of the action of the county commissioners that I am strongly identified with the Democratic Party; such is not the case. I never voted an out-and-out Democratic ticket in my life. I voted for Buchanan for President to defeat Fremont, but not because he was my first choice. In all other elections I have universally selected the candidates that, in my estimation, were the best fitted for the different offices; and it never happens that such men are all arranged on one side. The strongest friend I had in the Board of Commissioners is a Free Soiler; but opposition between parties is so strong that he would not vote for anyone, no matter how friendly, unless one at least of his own party would go with him. The Free Soil Party felt themselves bound to provide for one of their own party who was defeated for the office of county engineer."

In the same letter he writes of his family thus:

"Julia and the children are all well. Fred and Buck go to the school every day. They never think of asking to stay at home."

When the writer went abroad for the first time in an official capacity, the late William H. Seward, then Secretary of State, said to him jocosely and with a merry twinkle in his eye: "Consider every man a scoundrel until you have proved him to be honest." General Grant, on the other hand, considered every man honest until he proved him to be a scoundrel. The following incident is an illustration of this good trait in Grant's character; it is stated by himself in a letter to one of his brothers, dated Saint Louis, Mo., October 24, 1859:

"I have been postponing writing to you, hoping to make a return for your horse; but as yet I have received nothing for him. About two weeks ago a man spoke to me for him and said that he would try him the next day, and if he suited give me one hundred dollars for him. I have not seen the man since; but one week ago last Saturday he went to the stable and got the horse, saddle, and bridle; since which I have seen neither man nor horse. From this I presume he must like him. The man, I understand, lives in Florisant, about twelve miles from the city.

"P. S.—The man that has your horse is

Captain Covington, owner of a row of six three-story brick houses in this city; and the probabilities are that he intends to give me an order on his agent for the money on the first of the month, when the rents are paid. At all events, I imagine the horse is perfectly safe."

In reference to his employment, or rather want of employment, Grant writes in the same letter as follows:

"I am still unemployed, but expect to have a place in the customhouse on the first of next month. My name has been forwarded for the appointment of superintendent, which, if I do not get, will not probably be filled at all. In that case there is a vacant desk which I may get that pays twelve hundred dollars per annum. The other will be worth from fifteen hundred to eighteen hundred dollars, and will occupy but little time."

CHAPTER III.

At the Breaking Out of the War.

In the course of our conversation on the subject of his failure to obtain employment in Saint Louis, I asked the general whether he did not think that it was providential that every avenue of earning a livelihood in Saint Louis was closed against him, in order that he might be compelled to go where it would be easier for him to find an opening for re-entering the army at the outbreak of the war. He smiled and said, "Perhaps so." He fully believed in an overruling Providence. Indeed, I gathered from his remarks, made at different times, that he believed the fundamental doctrines of the Christian religion, and in the necessity of the Christian Church for the maintenance and advancement of moral and religious culture among the people. While he never made, previous to his last illness, so far as I know, a public profession of religion in the sense of what Methodists call conversion or regeneration, yet he believed in the reality of such "a change of heart" in many of his friends and acquaintances, among whom is his youngest sister Mary, of whose faith he said during his last illness: "I wish I had the strong faith that my sister Mary has." Before and after the war he was in the habit of attending public worship, usually at a Methodist church; for he was very fond of good and earnest preaching. On one occasion his sister Mary spoke in his presence of the Rev. Mr. Blank as being a good man, when, with a merry twinkle in his eye, he said, "Why, Mary, you speak of preachers as if their being good is an unusual thing."

General Grant was always an early riser. On the morning of the third day of his sojourn at my house in Copenhagen, before six o'clock, he entered my study, where I was engaged in my private devotion. Instead of withdrawing, he came and knelt at my side until its close. Whenever he had a clergyman as his guest, he always requested him to "say grace" at the table. During February, 1881, my wife and myself were his guests in New York. On the following Sunday morning we all attended church and heard an excellent sermon. On returning home, my wife asked him whether he would not like to have his second son to be a preacher? He replied, "Yes, if he could preach like Dr. ——."

After his failure to get any kind of employment in Saint Louis, Grant moved to Galena, Ill., where his father employed him as a clerk in his leather and findings store. (And here it may be proper to say that Grant never worked in his father's tannery, as has been so often stated by different writers and speakers.) One of his duties was to collect outstanding debts in various parts of the Northwest. I remember hearing his father say in reference to this subject that " Ulysses sometimes spent the amount he collected for horse and buggy hire," and that he "was not a great success as a collector." The general himself told me that this business was not to his liking, that he had no " faculty for dunning people;" and that, while he hated war, it was a relief to him to get back into the army. "When the war broke out," he said, " I felt it my duty to offer my services to the government that had educated me."

In reference to the raising of the first company of volunteers in Galena he wrote to his father, in a letter dated Camp Yates, near Springfield, May 6, 1861, as follows:

"At the time our first Galena company was raised I did not feel at liberty to engage in hot haste, but took an active interest in drilling them and imparting all the instruction I could, and at the request of the members of the company and of Mr. Washburn I came here for the purpose of assisting for a short time in camp, and, if necessary, giving my services for the war. The next two days after my arrival it was rainy and muddy, so that the troops could not drill, and I concluded to go home. Governor Yates heard of it, and requested me to remain. Since then I have been acting in that capacity, and for the last few days have been in command of this camp. The last of the six regiments called for from this State will probably leave by to-morrow or the day following, and then I shall be relieved from this command. The Legislature of this State provided for the raising of eleven additional regiments and a battalion of artillery, and a portion of these the governor will appoint me to muster into the service of the State, when I presume my services may end. I might have got the colonelcy of a regiment possibly; but I was perfectly sick of the political wire-pulling for all these commissions, and would not engage in it. I shall be no ways backward in offering my services when and where they are required; but I feel that I have done more now than I could do serving as captain under a green colonel; and if this thing continues, they will want more men at a later day. There have been full thirty thousand more volunteers offered their services than can be accepted under the present call, without including the call made by the State; but I can go back to Galena and drill the three or four companies there, and render them efficient for any future call. My own opinion is that this war will be but of short duration. The administration has acted most prudently and sagaciously so far in not bringing on a conflict before it had its forces fully marshaled. When they do strike, our thoroughly loyal States will be fully protected, and a few decisive victories in some of the Southern parts will send the secession army howling, and the leaders in the rebellion will flee the country. All the States will then be loyal for a generation to come; Negroes will depreciate so rapidly in value that nobody will want to own them, and their masters will be loudest in their declamation against the institution in a political and economical view. The Negro will never disturb the country again. The worst that is to be apprehended from him is now: he may revolt and cause more destruction than any Northern man wants to see. A Northern army may be required in the next ninety days to go South to suppress a Negro insurrection."

It appears from the above letter that Grant's early views about the duration of the war were similar to those of many other intelligent men. He told me that at that time he had no idea that the war would last longer than a few months. He, like others, had underrated the plans and determination of the Southern leaders of the rebellion, to say nothing of their Northern abettors, who then were as determined to divide the Union as their Southern friends.

With regard to Grant's offering his services to the government, he wrote, in a letter to his father, dated Galena, May 30, 1861, as follows:

"I have now been home nearly a week, but return to Springfield to-day. I have tendered my services to the government, and go to-day to make myself useful, if possible, from this until all our national difficulties are ended. During the six days I have been at home I have felt all the time as if a duty was being neglected that was paramount to any other duty I ever owed. I have every reason to be well satisfied with myself for the services already rendered, but to stop now would not do."

CHAPTER IV.

Grant's Promotion.

In his *Memoirs* Grant gives a description of what he did from the time of his return to Springfield, Ill., to July 3, when he wrote a letter to his father, dated Mexico, Mo., July 3, 1861, in which occurs the following concerning army matters as well as his promotion:

"The papers keep you posted as to army movements; and as you are already in possession of my notions on secession, nothing more is wanted on that point. I find here, however, a different state of feeling from what I expected to exist in any part of the South. The majority in this part of the State are secessionists, as we would term them, but deplore the present state of affairs. They would make almost any sacrifice to have the Union restored, but regard it as dissolved, and nothing is left for them but to choose between two evils. Many seem to be entirely ignorant of the object of present hostilities. You can't convince them but what the ultimate object is to extinguish, by force, slavery. Then, too, they feel that the Southern Confederacy will never consent to give up their State; and as they—the South—are the strong party, it is prudent to favor them from the start. There is never a movement of troops made that the secession journals throughout the country do not give a startling account of their almost annihilation at the hands of the State troops, while the facts are, there are no engagements. My regiment has been reported cut to pieces once that I know of, and I don't know but oftener, while a gun has not been fired at us. These reports go uncontradicted here, and give confirmation to the conviction already entertained, that one Southerner is equal to five Northerners. We believe that they are deluded, and know that if they are not, we are.

"Since I have been in command of this military district (two weeks) I have received the greatest hospitality and attention from the citizens about here. I have had every opportunity of conversing with them freely, and learning their sentiments; and although I have confined myself strictly to the truth as to what has been the result of the different engagements, the relative strength, etc., and the objects of the administration and the North generally, yet they don't believe a word, I think.

"I see from the papers that my name has been sent in for brigadier general. This is certainly very complimentary to me, particularly as I have never asked a friend to intercede in my behalf. My only acquaintance with men of influence in the

State was while on duty at Springfield, and I there saw so much pulling and hauling for favors that I determined never to ask for anything, and never have, not even a colonelcy. I wrote a letter to Washington, tendering my services, but they declined Governor Yates's and Mr. Trumbull's indorsement.

"My services with the regiment I am now with have been highly satisfactory to me. I took it in a very disorganized, demoralized, and insubordinate condition, and have worked it up to a reputation equal to the best; and, I believe, with the good will of all the officers and all the men. Hearing that I was likely to be promoted, the officers, with great unanimity, have requested to be attached to my command. This I do not want you to read to others, for I very much dislike speaking of myself.

"We are now breaking up camp here gradually. In a few days the last of us will be on our way for the Missouri River, at what point cannot be definitely determined, wood and water being a consideration as well as a healthy fine site for a large encampment."

CHAPTER V.

Grant's Busy Life—His Views on Religion.

IN the course of a conversation about fixedness of purpose and steadiness of perseverance in order to achieve success in life, Grant said that whatever he tried to do he always did it with all his might. He had no patience with lazy people. To live we must labor; must have something to do; some definite and fixed object in view, which shall be our means of support. He thought that strong, vigorous labor enables one to resist temptation and to do good; that there is happiness in the conscientious discharge of one's duties and in the achievement of success in whatever calling one may be engaged. But one must always have a definite purpose; for labor without it is scarcely better than none. According to his view success in life depends much upon fixedness of purpose and steadiness in perseverance. A man with no business, with nothing to do, is of no use to society; he is a consumer, but a nonproducer; hence a parasite.

Successful men, he thought, owe more to their perseverance than to their natural powers, or their friends, or favorable circumstances. Talent is desirable, but perseverance is more so; for it will strengthen the mental powers and intensify their energy. He said that according to his experience perseverance not only makes friends, but also favorable circumstances; that opposition, enemies, and barriers of every kind are gradually overcome by a stout heart and resolute energy of soul. He referred to Napoleon's resolution to make his way across the Alps as an example of what perseverance could accomplish.

When I referred to his own experiences in the war he said that he had always carried out what he had planned to do, though circumstances sometimes compelled him to change his original plan. I asked him if he ever thought he could not accomplish what he had set out to do or what was expected of him. He replied that he never thought of failure; that he continued his effort until he had accomplished his task.

To my question whether he ever prayed to God for assistance and success he replied that he often prayed to God mentally, but briefly, for strength and wisdom to enable him to carry to a successful termination the task expected of him. He further said that, like his mother, he never talked much about religion, but thought much on this all-important subject; that he believed in an overruling Providence; that the destiny of individuals and of nations is in God's hands; and that, while man has freedom of will and action, God overrules men's actions for the good of mankind. He further said that he could not see how anyone, in view of the history of the world, could be an atheist. To this I replied that I could not believe that there is really an atheist in the world, because religion, no matter what its form may be, in my opinion, is an innate, or an intuitive, or an original element of man's soul, and all religions presuppose a deity or deities of some kind or other. To this he replied, "I think your views are about right."

Apropos of the above remarks may be quoted what he wrote to his father about his busy life at the beginning of his career in the army at the outbreak of the war, in a letter dated Jefferson City, Mo., August 27, 1861:

"Your letter requesting me to appoint Mr. F. on my staff was only received last Friday, of course too late to give Mr. F. the appointment, even if I could do so. I remember to have been introduced to Mr. F., Sr., several years ago, and if the son is anything like the impression I then formed of the father the appointment would be one that I could well congratulate myself upon. I have filled all the places on my staff, and flatter myself with deserving men. . . . I only have one of them with me yet, and having all raw troops, and but little assistance, it keeps me busy from the time I get up in the morning until from twelve to two o'clock at night or morning.

"I have subscribed for the *Daily Democrat*, a stanch Union paper, for you, so that you might hear from me often. There is a good deal of alarm felt by citizens of an early attack upon this place; and if anything of the kind should take place we are illy prepared. All the troops are very raw, and about one half of them Missouri Home Guards without discipline. No artillery and but little cavalry are here.

"I do not anticipate an attack here myself; certainly not until we have attacked the enemy first. A defeat might induce he rebels to follow up their success to this point; but that we expect to prevent. My means of information are certainly as good as anyone else has, and I cannot learn that there is an organized body of men north of the Osage River, or any moving. There are numerous encampments through all the counties bordering on the Missouri River; but the object seems to be to gather supplies, horses, transportation, etc., for a fall and winter campaign.

"The country west of here will be left in a starving condition for the next winter. Families are being driven away in great numbers for their Union sentiments, leaving behind farms, crops, stock, and all. A sad state of affairs must exist under the most favorable circumstances that can take place. There will be no money in the country, and the entire crop will be carried off, together with all stock of any value.

"I am interrupted so often while writing that my letters must necessarily be very meager and disconnected."

CHAPTER VI.

Belmont—Our Country.

DURING the course of our conversations I asked the general about the engagement at or around Belmont. He narrated the affair substantially as we now find it described in his *Memoirs*. There is, however, a letter of his in existence which throws much new light on that subject. It is addressed to his father, part of which is copied from a letter addressed by the general to his wife. It reads *verbatim*, as follows:

"CAIRO, November 8, 1861.

"DEAR FATHER: It is late at night, and I want to get a letter into the mail for you before it closes. As I have just finished a very hasty letter to Julia that contains about what I would write, and having something else to do myself, I will have my clerk copy it on this [now follows the copy:

"Day before yesterday I left here with about three thousand men on five steamers, convoyed by two gunboats, and proceeded down the river to within about twelve miles of Columbus. The next morning the boats were dropped down just out of range of the enemy's batteries and the troops debarked.

"During this operation the gunboats exercised the rebels by throwing shells into their camps and batteries. When all ready we proceeded one mile toward Belmont, opposite Columbus, where I formed the troops into line, and ordered two companies from each regiment to deploy as skirmishers and push on through the woods and discover the position of the enemy. They had gone but a little way when they were fired upon, and the ball may be said to have fairly opened.

"The whole command, with the exception of a small reserve, were then deployed in like manner with the first, and ordered forward. The order was obeyed with great alacrity, the men all showing great courage. I can say with gratification that every colonel, without a single exception, set an example to their commands that inspired a confidence that will always insure victory, when there is the slightest possibility of gaining one. I feel truly proud to command such men. From here we fought our way from tree to tree through woods to Belmont, about two and a half miles, the enemy contesting every foot of ground. Here the enemy had strengthened their position by felling the trees for two or three hundred yards, and sharpening the limbs, making a sort of abatis. Our men charged through, making the victory complete, giving us possession of their camp and garrison, equipage, artillery, and everything else.

"We got a great many prisoners, the majority having succeeded in getting aboard their steamers and pushing across the river. We burned everything possible and started back, having accomplished all that we went for, and even more. Belmont is entirely covered by the batteries from Columbus, and is worth nothing as a military position; it cannot be held without Columbus.

"The object of the expedition was to prevent the enemy from sending a force into Missouri to cut off troops I had sent there for a special purpose, and to prevent reinforcing Price.

"Besides being well fortified at Columbus, their numbers far exceeded ours, and it would have been folly to have attacked them. We found the Confederates well armed and brave. On our return stragglers that had been left in our rear, now front, fired into us, and more recrossed the river and gave us battle for full a mile, and afterward at the boats when we were embarking. There was no hasty retreating or running away. Taking into account the object of the expedition, the victory was most complete. It has given me a confidence in the officers and men of this command that will enable me to lead them in any future engagement without fear of the result. General McClernand (who, by the way, acted with great coolness and courage throughout, and proved that he is a soldier as well as a statesman, and myself each had our horses shot from under us. Most of the field officers met with the same loss; besides, nearly one third of them being killed or wounded themselves. As near as I can ascertain, our loss was about two hundred and fifty killed, wounded, and missing. I write in great haste to get this in the office to-night."

The officers and men engaged in the battle of Belmont may well be proud of the well-merited praise given them by their commander. In conversing with me on that subject, he substantially repeated what he had written about it to his father. He further said that at no subsequent period during the war had he received greater encouragement by and confidence in his troops than by their courageous behavior at Belmont. If he had ever had doubts as to the courage, intelligence, and ability of the men called out from their civilian avocations to cope successfully with the rebellion, they were completely dissipated by the intelligence and courage displayed by his troops at Belmont.

He believed that these qualities were the result of true loyalty and ardent patriotism on the part of the soldiers and those of the loyal North that backed them. He had no patience with those who used the war for their own selfish ends,—for their enrichment at the expense of the country, or whose patriotism was measured by dollars and cents. These men, he thought, lacked a good conscience; or, if they had any, it was warped by their inordinate desire for gain. In a country like ours, he said, there is every possible inducement for cultivating true patriotism, and to give it its highest expression in noble deeds and gentlemanly behavior. We can and ought to make our country great by our being moral, intelligent, industrious, thrifty, if not religious; for everything that can be afforded by outward advantages, that the great Creator has given and the government or public may bestow, are in abundance around us. We have but to step in, and by intelligence, energy, and labor pluck the fruit of our endeavors.

He thought that our public-school system is excellent, most of our higher institutions of learning rest on solid foundations, their scholarship and sciences equal to those of other countries, our churches doing a good work for the public, our resources of all kinds enormous or incalculable, our mechanical skill unrivaled, and our literature, so far as he was able to judge, on the whole, good; hence we ought to love our country, do all in our power to maintain the Union and advance its interests in every direction. He thought that our children had good and inspiring examples in the lines and deeds of those noble men and women who have made our country what it is, and thus far maintained its integrity and placed it in a path of achieving "still greater greatness."

CHAPTER VII.

Grant's Conscientiousness.

GENERAL GRANT insisted everywhere and always on conscientiousness, and everyone who knew him was aware that he himself was extremely conscientious in everything he said and did. The love of truth and right was a conspicuous quality of his character. It was the spring-source of his integrity. He fully believed the sentiment that "an honest man is the noblest work of God." It was this sentiment that crowned him with real nobility. He also believed in the truth of the sentiment of the German philosopher Kant: "The two most beautiful things in the universe are, the starry heavens above us, and the sense of duty within us." This sense of duty in Grant was inspired by his conscientiousness. The idea of obligation, responsibility, faithfulness to trust, rectitude, justice, right—all these qualities were highly developed in him. Anyone who had the privilege of listening to his conversations in the privacy of the family circle or among intimate friends must have noticed that these qualities were prominent in his character. It pained him to see a lack of them in others, and he exacted them from those who served under him.

An illustration of the truth of the above statement is found in the following letter addressed to his father:

"CAIRO, ILL., November 28, 1861.

"DEAR FATHER: Your letter asking if Mr. L. can be passed South, and also inclosing two extracts from papers, is received.

"It is entirely out of the question to pass persons South. We have many Union men sacrificing their lives now from exposure as well as in battle in a cause brought about by secession, and it is necessary for the security of the thousands still exposed that all communication should be cut off between the two sections.

"As to that article in the *Hawk-Eye*, it gives me no uneasiness whatever. The Iowa regiment has done its duty fully, and my report gives it full credit. All who were on the battlefield know where General McClernand and myself were, and it needs no resort to the public press for our vindication. The other extract gives our loss in killed and wounded almost exactly correct; our missing, however, is only three or four over one hundred. Recent information received through deserters shows that the rebel loss from killed, wounded, and missing reaches about two thousand five hundred. One thing is certain, after the battle one third of Columbus was used for hospitals, and many were removed to houses in the country. There were also two steamboat loads sent to Memphis, and the largest hotel in the city was taken as a hospital. The city was put in mourning and all business suspended for a day and the citizens thrown into the greatest consternation lest they would be attacked."

The first few years of the war General Grant was frequently attacked or mercilessly criticised by a portion of the public press, probably arising from a want of knowledge of all the facts of the case in hand. His father was worried about it and wanted to defend him, or get others to do so; but he would never engage in newspaper controversy in his own defense, nor permit others to do so if he could help it. In his conversation with me on this subject he said that ordinarily he hated newspaper controversy, that he was always willing to be judged by his actions as well as by the reports he sent to the government of his operations in the field. He believed that some of the generals of the late war were "puffed" by newspaper correspondents either into obscurity, or "to the rear," or "out of their command." While some commanding officers had newspaper correspondents on their personal staffs, who wrote flattering reports about their doings, he never employed one on his staff, and would hardly tolerate one even in his camp. This, he believed, was one of the reasons why some of the newspapers frequently attacked or mercilessly criticised him, and had seldom anything good to say about him. He believed that "right is might," and that right and truth will ultimately triumph. He disliked to talk or write about himself, or to talk against others. This is a trait of character of the Grant family. The following incident will illustrate it:

On one occasion the ladies' benevolent society of the church of which Mother Grant was a member met at her house for the purpose of making some garments for the wife and children of a drunkard who consumed all his earnings by drink. The subject of their conversation, among other things, was the vile character of said drunkard. According to their remarks there was not a single redeeming trait left in that man. When all had had their "say-so," Mother Grant looked up and said, "Well, Mr. A. was a good fiddler, anyhow."

I never heard Mother Grant nor the general say an unkind thing against anybody. If the latter ever made a criticism upon anyone, it was always confined within the strict limits of truth.

The following letter from the general to his father, who was worried by some attacks made upon the former, will illustrate his aversion to self-defense in newspapers. It is dated "Corinth, Miss., August 3, 1862," and contains, among other things, the following remarks:

"You must not expect me to write in my own defense, nor to permit it from anyone about me. I know that the feeling of the troops under my command is favorable to me, and so long as I continue to do my duty faithfully it will remain so. . . . I do not expect, nor want, the support of the ——— city press on my side. Their course has been so remarkable from the beginning, that should I be indorsed by them, I should fear that the public would mistrust my patriotism. I am sure that I have but one desire in this war, and that is to put down the rebellion. I have no 'hobby' of my own with regard to the Negro. If Congress passes any law and the President approves it I am willing to execute it. Laws are certainly as binding on the minority as on the majority. I do not believe even in the discussion of the propriety of laws and official orders by the army. One enemy is enough at a time, and when he is subdued it will be time enough to settle personal differences.

"I do not want to command a department, because I believe I can do better service in the field. I do not expect to be overslaughed by a junior, and should feel exceedingly mortified should such a thing occur, but would keep quiet, as I have ever done heretofore."

CHAPTER VIII.

Grant's Views on Slavery—How he was Brought Forward as a Presidential Candidate.

THE following letters will explain themselves, as they relate to army matters:

"CORINTH, MISS., August 19, 1862.

"DEAR SISTER: I am now in a situation where it is impossible for me to do more than to protect my long lines of defense. I have the Mississippi to Memphis, the railroad from Columbus to Corinth, from Jackson to Bolivar, from Corinth to Decatur, and the Tennessee and Cumberland rivers to keep open. Guerrillas are hovering around in every direction, getting whipped every day at some place by some of my command, but keeping us busy. The war is evidently getting oppressive to the Southern people. Their "institution" are beginning to have ideas of their own, and every time an expedition goes out more or less of them follow in the wake of the army and come into camp. I am using them as teamsters, hospital attendants, company cooks, etc., thus saving soldiers to carry the musket. I don't know what is to become of these poor people in the end, but it is weakening the enemy to take them from them. If the new levies are sent in soon the rebels will have a good time getting in their crops this fall.

"I have abandoned all hope of being able to make a visit home before the close of the war. A few weeks' recreation would be very grateful, however. It is one constant strain now, and has been for a year. If I do get through I think I will take a few months of pure and undefiled rest. I stand it well, however, having gained some fifteen pounds in weight since leaving Cairo."

The general's reference in the above letter to the peculiar "institution"—that is, to the status of the Negro at the time it was written—leads me to state his opinion concerning it from the time he entered the army until Congress busied itself with the reconstruction of the Southern States.

General Grant was originally not an abolitionist. He believed in letting slavery alone, though he was far from believing it to be a "divine institution." He believed that Mr. Lincoln's course in reference to it previous to the declaration of emancipation was right; nor did he object to the emancipation of the slaves. He did, however, privately object at first to the their enfranchisement before they were able to read and write. But when the reconstruction acts had been put into operation and the Kuklux endeavored to suppress the political rights of the freedmen of the South by the use of unscrupulous means, etc., he, as the head of the army, became convinced by the reports of those who had to aid in suppressing "Kukluxism" that the ballot was the only real means the freedmen had for defending their lives, property, and rights. When President Johnson came into conflict with Congress on the questions of the Freedmen's Bureau and the reconstruction acts, the general took a decisive stand in favor of the congressional legislation on those great national questions, though he refrained from talking openly on the subject. I remember, being his guest in Washington at the time, how he prefaced his remarks, in the privacy of the family, relative to this matter with the words, "Now, what I am going to say I do not want to be printed in the newspapers." He believed it to be improper for army officers to discuss or criticise congressional legislation. "We are here to execute, not to criticise, the acts of Congress," he said. Hence, neither senators nor representatives really knew his sentiments on these topics; nor were they able to "pump" them out of him. As the head of the army he refused to talk on politics, desiring thus to set a good example in this matter to his subordinate officers.

When there was "talk" of bringing him forward as the Republican candidate for the presidency the leaders of the party hesitated, for they were not quite sure whether Grant was a Republican or a Democrat. It was known that he had voted for Buchanan as President; and this fact, together with his silence on the reconstruction acts, made these leaders doubt his genuine Republicanism (in the party sense of the term).

It was some time during the early spring of 1867 that Senator Wade came to Covington, Ky. (where General Grant's father resided), for the purpose of calling on the latter to inquire of him what the general's sentiments were in reference to the great questions that agitated Congress at that time. Both Father and Mother Grant were out, and so, too, were the other members of the family, except myself (my wife and myself were at that time residing with her parents).

Senator Wade was disappointed. He was about to leave, when I said, "Senator Wade, perhaps I can tell you what you wish to know." He asked, "Who are you?" I replied, "I am Mr. Cramer, Father and Mother Grant's son-in-law." He said, "Perhaps you can tell me what I want to know. I want to know what General Grant's sentiments are with regard to the action of Congress relative to the Freedmen's Bureau, the reconstruction acts, etc.; in short, I want to know whether he is a good Republican; for we desire to bring him forward as our candidate for the presidency; yet we do not exactly know where he stands on these questions." "Well," I replied, "I know General Grant's sentiments on all these great questions; for I was his guest during

February last, and heard him express his opinions freely on all measures proposed and adopted by Congress; but he then exacted a promise from me that what he was 'about to say was not to go to the press.' If you will promise me not to betray the name of your informant I will give you all the information you want."

After having received his promise I told him that General Grant indorsed all congressional measures; that he was a thorough Republican, and that the Republican Party could as fully trust Grant as it trusted him (the senator). I then proceeded to give him in detail what I had heard the general say in reference to the different acts of Congress respecting the freedmen and the reconstruction of the Southern States, etc. When I had ended my remarks Senator Wade rose from his chair, threw his slouch hat toward the ceiling (breaking a globe of the chandelier), and exclaimed: "That settles the matter;

we shall propose Grant as the candidate of the Republican Party for the presidency. I am greatly relieved. The whole party will rejoice with me that we are relieved of this terrible uncertainty and have found our presidential candidate. With him we are sure to win. I thank you for this long-desired information."

Senator Wade returned to Cincinnati. He faithfully kept his promise; for, so far as I was able to learn, he never mentioned my name in connection with his communicating the information I had given him to others. In the summer of 1869 I met him again; he recognized me and thanked me again for the information I had given him in the early spring of 1867, and with a smile he said, "You see what has come of it."

During the time the general was my guest in Copenhagen I took occasion to tell him that once, and only once, I had "betrayed his confidence," and then I narrated to him the story of Senator Wade's call at his father's house in Covington, Ky. "Well," said Grant, "I never heard of it; but I think it was all right. It did not get into the papers; but (with a smile) how did you prevent it?" I told him that I had exacted a promise from Wade not to mention my name in connection with the information he had received from me, nor to have our interview published in the newspapers. "Well, general," said I, "will you pardon my 'betrayal' of your confidence in this matter?" With a merry twinkle in his eye and a smile on his lips he replied: "How can I, after having experienced the consequences of your 'betrayal;' but I guess it is all right." "I am glad," I said, "for a number of reasons that you have never heard of this incident before." "I am glad, too," he said, "that you never asked for a reward for it." I replied: "It has never occurred to me that I had done anything in this matter that deserved a reward. All I did was to relieve Senator Wade of an uncertainty in reference to your political sentiments at a critical time when Congress and the President were at loggerheads with each other, and when it behooved every loyal and patriotic citizen legitimately to do all in his power to bring about a pacific settlement of the difficulties growing out of the late war."

"It would be a good thing for our country," he said, "if all our people could see and do their duties in that light; but I am sorry to say there is a good deal of self-seeking among some of our politicians, who expect and demand a reward for every little service they render, not so much for the country as for their party, and generally they do not always belong to the best class of citizens. A truly loyal and patriotic citizen performs his duties as a citizen, not with the expectation of receiving a reward for it, except the reward of a good conscience, but because he loves his country and desires to promote its best interests. Didn't Christ say somewhere that if we have done our duties we are still unprofitable servants for merely having done what we ought to have done?"

I replied: "Yes; the exact words of Christ are: 'When ye shall have done all those things which are commanded you, say, We are unprofitable servants: we have done that which was our duty to do.' I take this to mean in our case that, as the citizen receives from the State protection of life and family and property, and many other privileges and blessings, he is bound in return to perform his duties to the State, whatever they may be, which is really nothing more than giving a *quid pro quo;* hence he has no right to claim a reward as if he had rendered the State an extraordinary service. A child receiving protection, support, education, and love from its parents is in duty bound to render them in return loving obedience, and has no right to claim an extra reward as though it had rendered them some extraordinary service. This, I think, expresses in principle the relation between the State and the citizen, as well as the doctrine of the justification of the sinner by grace alone; if the sinner is thus justified by God, then the obligation of the sinner to love and serve God in return grows naturally out of this fact, and he has no right to claim an extra reward for love and service thus rendered."

"Ah," replied the general, "you are getting into the field of theology; but I think your explanation and application are correct. If only some of our politicians could be made to see it in that light; but I have known men who claimed appointments from me because they had voted for me. I cannot imagine how some people can do such a thing. Is it not enough that they have the right to vote for whom they please? Is it not preposterous for men to claim a reward for having exercised that right—a right freely given to them by the State? Such people ought to learn the first principles of moral philosophy, to say nothing of the teachings of Christ. I have had a good opportunity to notice much of the selfishness of human nature, and the thought occurred to me that the children in our public schools ought to be instructed in the principles of moral philosophy; of course, this instruction should be adapted to their understanding, for there are many children and parents who do not attend church or Sunday school, and some of the former generally grow up without having correct ideas of right and wrong, of duty, service, submission, trade, commerce, etc. While we cannot compel parents and children to attend church and Sunday school (which is one of the glories of our country), yet the State should see to it that the children attending our public schools should receive instruction in the science of morals, so that they may become intelligent citizens, having correct ideas of the laws and rules that govern the relations of parents and children, of citizens and the State, of citizens to each other, etc. This would be one of the strongest measures for securing good citizens as well as for perpetuating our form of government and making our nation really great."

CHAPTER IX.

Some Wartime Letters.

THE following extracts from two letters written by the general, the one from "Corinth, Miss.," and the other from "Oxford, Miss.," will explain themselves. The reason why the letters are not given entire is that portions of them contain private or family matters that are not of public interest. The first one is addressed to his father, dated:

"CORINTH, MISS., September 17, 1862.

"DEAR FATHER: A letter from you and one from Mary were received some time ago, which I commenced to answer in a letter addressed to Mary, but being frequently interrupted by matters of business it was laid aside for some days and finally torn up. I now have all my time taxed. Although occupying a position attracting but little attention at this time, there is probably no garrison more threatened than this. I expect to hold it, and have never had any other feeling, either here or elsewhere, but that of success."

[Here follows a request to his father not to do anything in the way of defending him against the attacks of the press, which, as was usual, worried his father a good deal, and prompted him to take up the pen, or get others to do so, in defense of his son, for whose success he was naturally very anxious. The general wrote him :]

"I require no defenders. . . . Persons who have returned to this army said that they found the best of feeling existing toward me in every place except in Cincinnati. Do nothing to correct anything, and keep quiet on this subject.

"Mary wrote me about an appointment for Mr. N. I have nothing in the world to do with any appointments, no power to make, and nothing to do with recommending except for my own staff. That is now already full."

Parts of the other letter, addressed to his sister Mary, read as follows:

"OXFORD, MISS., December 15, 1862.

"DEAR SISTER: Yesterday I received a letter from you and the children and one from Uncle Samuel. . . . I shall remain here to-morrow, or the next day at farthest.

"We are now having wet weather. I have a big army in front of me as well as bad roads. I shall probably give a good account of myself, however, notwithstanding all obstacles. My plans are all complete for weeks to come, and I hope to have them all work out just as planned. For a conscientious person, and I profess to be one, this is a most slavish life. I may be envied by ambitious persons, but I in turn envy the person who can transact his daily business and retire to a quiet home without the feeling of responsibility for to-morrow. Taking my whole department, there are an immense number of lives staked upon my judgment and acts. I am extended now like a peninsula into an enemy's country with a large army depending for their daily bread upon keeping open a line of railroad running one hundred and ninety miles through an enemy's country, or at least through territory occupied by a people terribly embittered and hostile to us. With all this I suffer the mortification of seeing myself attacked right and left by people at home professing patriotism and love of country who never heard the whistle of a hostile bullet. I pity them and a nation dependent upon such for its existence. I am thankful, however, that although such people make a great noise, the masses are not like them.

"To all my other trials I have to contend against is added that of speculators whose patriotism is measured by dollars and cents. Country has no value with them compared with money. To elucidate this would take quires of paper, so I will reserve this for an evening's conversation if I should be so fortunate as to again get home, where I can have a day to myself.

"Tell the children to learn their lessons, mind their grandma, and be good children. I should like very much to see them. To me they are all obedient and good. I may be partial, but they seem to me to be children to be proud of."

Speaking here of his children, the general had reference to the fact that they were for the time being staying at his parents' home in Covington, Ky., where they went to school, and were for some time under the care and management of the general's mother and sisters. According to the first part of the above letter his wife and father were at the time of writing at Holly Springs for the purpose of paying him a visit. The general had always been very fond of his children and had a high opinion of their character and ability. He was very "domestic" in his habits and tastes. He loved to be at home, surrounded by his family. He did not believe in physical punishment as applied to children. He told me that, so far as his children were concerned, he put them "on their honor," and he believed it had a better effect than if he had applied physical punishment to them. This thought is worthy of the attention of parents and educators.

It is evident from the above letter that the general was very sensitive in reference to the attacks made upon him by the press and others at home while he was at the front doing all in his power to put down the rebellion, denying himself of home comforts and the presence of his family, and bearing day and night an awful responsibility for the support of his army in the enemy's country, as well as for their and his honor in prosecuting the war successfully and meeting the expectations of the government and the people. In conversing on this subject at a subsequent period he told me that though he bore it all in silence he was frequently discouraged and felt tempted to resign his commission and go home. He thought it ungenerous, to say the least, on the part of those who attacked him to charge him with things of which he was not guilty, and to criticise his plans and actions when they were totally ignorant of the position and circumstances of the case, while he was at the front bearing all the hardships, privations, and responsibility, and they at their homes enjoying their comforts and rest and ease, with no responsibility whatsoever connected with the war. But being conscientious, and knowing that he was doing his very best under the circumstances, he could afford to wait until time justified his course. His detracters are forgotten, or nearly so, while his name still lives and is honored.

A great trial to him were those "speculators whose patriotism was then measured by dollars and cents," and who thought more of money-making than of their country in distress. He told me that he was often besieged by them, requesting him to give them "passes" to go South; and in some cases he was even requested to give them a military guard for protection—a thing he never did. Of course, these disappointed "speculators" returned home and caused "complaints" and "charges," manufactured out of whole cloth, to be circulated and published against him in a portion of the press that was either opposed to the prosecution of the war, or whose "correspondents" he did not appoint on his staff nor furnish with news from headquarters. These complaints and charges, coming from men who had "recently been at the front," were made to have the semblance of truth and thus to hurt the general, if they were not intended to be the means for his removal. Seen and judged at this distance, these men were worse than the rebels; for the latter fought for their "cause," and thus staked their lives and property in its maintenance or defense, while the former endeavored to take advantage of their bleeding country to enrich themselves at its expense; and if the commanding general felt it to be his duty to put his veto upon their selfish, if not unlawful, endeavors, they, in a cowardly manner, stabbed him in the back.

CHAPTER X.

Before the Fall of Vicksburg.

"WALNUT HILLS, MISS., June 15, 1863.

"DEAR FATHER: I have received several letters from Mary and yourself, but, as I have to do with nineteen-twentieths of those received, have neglected to answer them.

"All I can say is that I am well; I have the enemy closely hemmed in all around. My position is naturally strong and fortified against an attack from outside. I have been so strongly reinforced that Johnston will have to come with a mighty host to drive me away. I do not look upon the fall of Vicksburg as in the least doubtful. If, however, I could have carried the place on the twenty-second of last month I could by this time have made a campaign that would have made the State of Mississippi almost safe for a solitary horseman to ride over. As it is, the enemy have a large army in it, and the season has so far advanced that water will be difficult to find for an army marching, besides the dust and heat that must be encountered. The fall of Vicksburg now will only result in the opening of the Mississippi River and the demoralization of the enemy. I intended more from it; I did my best, however, and, looking back, can see no blunder committed. Yours, etc., ULYSSES."

Having always been naturally interested in what led to the siege and the taking of Vicksburg (having a brother killed in the battle of Champion's Hill), I asked the general about it, and he narrated substantially the affair as we find it described in his *Memoirs*, only not quite so elaborately; and he made the identical remarks found in Vol. I, pp. 519, 520: "Had McClernand come up with reasonable promptness, or had I known the ground as I did afterward, I cannot see how Pendleton could have escaped with any organized force;" hence on June 15, 1863, he could write to his father, "Looking back I can see no blunder committed," meaning on his own part. But he expressed regrets that General McClernand did not move more rapidly, as in that case Vicksburg would have fallen at least a month earlier into his hands. What would have been the consequence of this cannot be calculated with exactness; but in Grant's opinion it would probably have shortened the war and hastened the restoration of peace.

CHAPTER XI.

Grant Declines a Civil Office.

FROM the following letter it appears that General Grant was urged to be a candidate for a certain office not mentioned therein. It is probable that the men whose names are mentioned in it suggested to his father and to himself the propriety of his allowing his name to be brought forward as a candidate for the Presidency, though I am not quite sure about it. The letter will explain itself:

"NASHVILLE, TENN., February 20, 1864.

"DEAR FATHER: I have received your letter and those accompanying it, to-wit: Mr. Newton's and J. N. Morris's. I may write to Mr. Newton, but it will be different from what he expects. I am not a candidate for any office. All I want is to be left alone to fight this war out, fight all rebel opposition, and restore a happy Union in the shortest possible time. You know, or ought to know, that the public prints are not the proper mediums through which to let a personal feeling pass. I know that I feel that nothing personal to myself could ever induce me to accept a political office.

"Judging from your letter you seem to have taken an active feeling, to say the least, in this matter, that I would like to talk to you about it. I could write, but do not want to do so. Why not come down here and see me?

"Yours, etc., ULYSSES."

General Grant never conversed with me on this subject, except to say that while in the army he had been requested to "run for an office;" that he peremptorily declined to do so; that he never had a desire while in the army for a political office, not even for the presidency; that he was perfectly satisfied with being in the army, and that after the war it was his intention to spend the remainder of his life, or until he had reached the legal limit, in the position as head of the army. He told me that it cost him a severe struggle to accept the nomination as candidate for the presidency offered to him by the Republican Party in 1868, and that only upon the strogu presentation of the case by the leaders of that party, and taking the situation and circumstances into consideration, he felt it his duty to obey that call and serve his country in the position to which the people afterward elected him. He said that when the people, through their representatives, called him to any position, he felt it his duty to obey that call, whatever his personal feelings or his likes and dislikes might be. When the country calls a citizen to perform any service it is his duty to obey, "though," he said, with a smile, "there are some who either call themselves, or by some hook or crook get others to call them, and then they boast that the country has called them."

Upon another occasion he said to me: "I can truly say that I never sought the presidency, nor any promotion that came to me in the army during the war. They all came to me unsolicited; but in all positions that thus came to me I endeavored to do my duty as I saw it, conscientiously, and to give satisfaction to those who promoted or elected me. From the time my services were accepted in 1861 until the expiration of my second term as President I never asked for promotion, nor got others to ask for me. Perhaps one reason why I received unsolicited promotions is that I never allowed myself to deviate from the path of duty—from what was given me to do. I never aspired to hold any political office; I never sought newspaper 'puffs' or influence. My sole desire was to do all in my power to put down the rebellion and restore the Union. While I was in the army I never criticised the actions of Congress or of the administration; I simply obeyed all the orders given me by my superiors. I may say I was a man of one purpose, namely, to put down the rebellion."

CHAPTER XII.

Grant's Views on President Lincoln, Stanton, Seward, Chase, and Johnson.

IN this connection it may be well to give an extract from a letter addressed to his father relative to a certain young man (Mr. W.) in the army, who appears at that time to have been undergoing punishment for an offense, but who had the audacity to apply for a position on the general's staff. It is as follows:

"CULPEPPER COURT HOUSE, VA., April 16, 1864.

"DEAR FATHER: Your letter inclosing one from young W., asking for duty on my staff during his suspension, is received. It is the third letter from him on the same subject. Of course, I cannot gratify him. It would not be proper. It would be changing punishment into reward. . . .

"It has rained here almost every day since my arrival; it is still raining. Of course, I say nothing of when the army moves, or how, or where. I am in most excellent health, and well pleased with appearances here. Yours, etc.,

"ULYSSES."

The general's remarks relative to young W. show his high sense of propriety and justice. He told me that this was not the first time that similar requests were made of him by persons (or their friends) who were either undergoing some kind of punishment for having committed some offense or were known to entertain favorable feelings for the Southern cause, but who coveted the distinction of serving on General Grant's staff irrespective of their merit or ability, or both. Whenever he had received promotion applications for positions on his staff came pouring in from all classes of men, some known and some unknown to him, who cared less for rendering real service, but more for the honor it would bring to them.

The letter written from Culpepper Court House soon after the general had assumed command of the armies of the United States, and making his headquarters with the Army of the Potomac, suggests a remark he made to me relative to his directing the movements of that army. He said that, the army being so near Washington, he was afraid lest senators and members of Congress might endeavor to interfere with his plans, and thus bring confusion into or retard the movements of the army; that therefore he had requested President Lincoln to see to it that such should not be the case, and that he had received the desired assurance. Continuing to speak of Mr. Lincoln, he said that he never knew a man in a high position who had the faculty to manage other men so easily and without giving offense in such a high degree as he.

While he was gentle and humane, he was nevertheless decisive in his opinions. He was very careful of the feelings of others and approachable to all classes of persons. He was morally and intellectually great without assuming to be great, and had the gift of easily comprehending any situation with which he had to deal. He was always governed by the best of motives, and was thoroughly unselfish. The country was fortunate in having him as President during the most trying period in its history. No man could have done better, if as well. He will be more thought of as time passes. He will go down into history as one of the greatest men America has ever produced.

Concerning Mr. Stanton, Secretary of War under Mr. Lincoln, General Grant said that he was also a great man in his way, and the right man in the right place; that few, if any could have done as well in the War Office during the war as he did, but he had not the same ability of managing men that Mr. Lincoln had; that he was not as considerate of the feelings of others as Mr. Lincoln was; that he had a strong will, that in great emergencies he was uneasy and fidgety; still, in the War Office he was the complement of Mr. Lincoln.

With reference to William H. Seward, Secretary of State, Grant said that he considered him a great statesman; that he managed our foreign affairs during the war with consummate skill; that Mr. Lincoln could not have had a better man in that office than Mr. Seward was; and that he rendered our country an immense service by preventing war between the United States and England while yet maintaining our rights. He also praised Seward's diplomatic skill in inducing Napoleon III to withdraw his troops from Mexico, thus preventing the establishment of a permanent empire in our neighborhood.

Relative to S. P. Chase, Secretary of the

Treasury, the general said, that he always admired his great financial ability; that by his skillful management of our national finances during the war he rendered the country an immense service; that his honesty and integrity were never questioned, though he might easily have enriched himself; that he was a thoroughbred gentleman, possessing a great mind, a great character, and great statesmanship. His weakness consisted chiefly in his inordinate ambition to become President, which induced him to seek the Democratic nomination. The nobility of Mr. Lincoln's character, he said, is shown, among other things, in nominating Mr. Chase, in October, 1864, to the Senate for the position of Chief Justice of the Supreme Court of the United States after he had been seeking during that year the nomination for the Presidency in the place of Mr. Lincoln.

Concerning Andrew Johnson, Grant said that while he was naturally smart and shrewd he nevertheless showed the defectiveness of his early education; that in some things he was stubborn, and mistook it for strength of character; that his denunciations of the rebels, after he had become President, caused a great deal of uneasiness and trouble in the South; that the sudden change in his sentiments respecting the Southern States brought him into conflict with Congress and did a great deal of harm; and that he was ambitious and designing for a second term. That strange charm and nobility so manifest in Mr. Lincoln's character was absent in Mr. Johnson's. There were no revengeful feelings in Mr. Lincoln; if there were he never showed them; but Mr. Johnson was revengeful, passionate, and opinionated. "While Mr. Johnson had some good traits in his character, yet as a whole I cannot admire him."

Of the two Congresses that carried on the war, Grant had nothing but good to say. He admired their patriotism and the unstinted liberality with which they voted men and means to prosecute the war to its close. "Without their active support," he said, "we would have failed in suppressing the rebellion."

CHAPTER XIII.

Much to Do—Little Influence—Grant's Views on Providence.

THE following extracts from letters addressed to his father, one at the close of the war, and the other nearly three years later, will show the general's busy life during and after the war; and that he possessed apparently little influence in getting appointments for applicants:

"HEADQUARTERS ARMIES OF THE U. S.,
"WASHINGTON, May 6, 1865.

"DEAR FATHER: I have just returned from Philadelphia, leaving Mr. Cramer there. He can describe our new house to you when he returns.

"My health is good, but I find so much to do that I can scarcely keep up with public business, let alone answering all the private letters I receive. My going to Philadelphia and spending half my time there, as I hope to do, will give me some leisure. I attend to public business there by telegraph and avoid numerous calls taking up much time, or hope to do so. . . .

"I hope to hear of mother's entire recovery. Yours, etc. ULYSSES."

"HEADQUARTERS ARMIES OF THE U. S.,
WASHINGTON, February 10, 1868.

"DEAR FATHER: I spoke to Secretary McCulloch about giving Mrs. P. a clerkship in the Treasury, and he promised me he would do it, but has not yet done it. Now, I fancy I have not much influence, and if I had I would be very careful about using it. The family are well and send much love to mother, Jennie, and yourself.

"Yours truly, U. S. GRANT."

The Mrs. P. referred to in the above letter was the widow of an army officer who was killed in the war and left her and her boy without any means. She resided in Covington, Ky., and made application through the general's father for a clerkship in the Treasury Department. She never got it, which induced him to say that "he had not much influence," and even if he had he "would be very careful about using it."

The house referred to in the first of the above letters was the one donated to him by the citizens of Philadelphia soon after the close of the war. It was a fine, commodious house, with all the modern improvements and conveniences. With becoming modesty and sincere gratitude he accepted it as a token of the appreciation, on the part of the citizens of that city, of the services he was enabled, "with the help of the armies of the United States, to render our country." It was then his intention to let his family reside there, while he divided his time between Philadelphia and Washington, but the business of his office incident to the disbanding of the armies of the United States at the close of the war, and the reorganization of the regular army, etc., was so enormous that he was compelled soon to abandon his plan and move his family to Washington. It was fortunate, however, that his attention had been directed to Philadelphia immediately after the close of the war; otherwise he would probably have been in Washington at the time of the assassination of Mr. Lincoln and the attack upon Mr. Seward and his son. In all probability he would have shared the same fate. It was no doubt a merciful Providence that thus enabled him to escape the hand of the assassin; at least he told me, when we conversed on the assassination of Mr. Lincoln, that he looked upon it as such, "for I am," he said, "a profound believer in a special and a general providence that shapes the destiny of individuals and nations."

We had several conversations on this subject. To illustrate : At the outbreak of the war he was somewhat indifferent to the question of the abolition of slavery. He thought at first that the rebellion could be suppressed without its abolition. But as the war progressed he became gradually convinced that "slavery was doomed and must go." He had always recognized its moral evil, as also its being the cause of the war; and "as all evil must be punished in some form at some time, and as nations have no organized existence hereafter, they must be punished here for their national sins;" hence General Grant came to look upon the war as a divine punishment for the sin of slavery; and God used human beings to carry out his purposes. "Thus," he said, "we see a special providence that shapes the calling and destiny of individuals, and we see a general providence that governs nations, yet all in such a way as not to destroy man's free agency." Grant was communicative to me on religious and Church matters whenever I broached these subjects. Few Christians were more conscientious and just than he was.

CHAPTER XIV.

Office-seeking an Industry.

THE following letter, addressed to his sister Mary, will be read with interest:

"WASHINGTON, D. C., March 31, 1869.

"MY DEAR SISTER: I received a note from you a few days since which ought to have been answered at once. The fact is, however, that I scarcely get one moment alone. Office-seeking in this country, I regret to say, is getting to be one of the industries of the age. It gives me no peace. With the adjournment of Congress, however, I hope it will be better.

"Father and Jennie left here last Thursday after a visit of several weeks. You heard, no doubt, that father got a severe fall on inauguration day. He is not much improved, and I fear never will entirely recover. It is not probable that his injury will shorten his life, but will probably make him lame for life. He had but little peace while here. Office-seekers were after him from breakfast till bedtime. . . .

"The family are all well and join me in love. Yours truly, U. S. GRANT."

General Grant told me on one occasion that during the time of his settlement in Washington after the war and his inauguration he had an inkling of the extent to which office-seeking is carried on in this country, having been frequently requested, both in letters and *viva voce*, by persons known and unknown to him, to intercede in their behalf with the "powers that be" for the purpose of securing offices for them, but in comparison with what he experienced in this line after his inauguration it was as a little flowing brook to the mighty cataract of Niagara. Is it a wonder that he calls office-seeking "one of the industries of the age?" Here were, in the first place, the Republican senators and representatives, who claimed the first consideration; then there came friends and acquaintances who believed that they had a primary claim upon him for themselves or their friends or relatives; then came governors of States and officers of the army and navy, and lastly a host of unknown persons, some of whom brought letters of introduction or recommendation from friends or politicians, while others came in their own name. "The whole business," he said, "was simply overwhelming." For each of the hundreds or thousands of appointments there were from ten to twenty, and even more, applicants. Of course, the majority of the office-seekers had to be disappointed.

To illustrate: It appears from the above letter that Father Grant was also daily besieged with the importunities of many office-seekers, whether he was at his own home or at his son's in Washington. From 1867 to 1870 I was consul at Leipzig. From the time it had been officially declared that Grant was elected President of the United States until the first of May following—that is, during less than five months—I received not less than one hundred and fifty-three written applications for different offices, domestic and foreign, with the request that I should indorse and forward them to the President, accompanied by a personal letter from me to him. During the said month of May I came home on a leave of absence, and, spending a week at the White House, I, like Father Grant, was daily besieged by office-seekers, and this thing followed me to New York and Covington, Ky., during the whole of my leave of absence.

More than this: Certain parties—whiskey distillers—approached me and offered me several hundred thousand dollars "if I would go to Washington, reside there, and keep on 'good terms' with the Commissioner of Internal Revenue." I simply replied, "Thy money perish with thee" (Acts viii, 20). At that time gold was above par, and hence, in a certain sense, an article of merchandise. The government sold gold coin or bullion as it was needed by bankers or importers, etc. Certain other parties approached me and offered me large sums of money if "I would reside in Washington and procure for them the first information when the government would throw gold upon the market." Knowing what they wanted, I replied, "Gentlemen, I have no right to trade with President Grant's name," and, as in the other case, I walked away.

These incidents are mentioned here to corroborate Grant's statement, that "office-seeking has become one of the industries of the age." There are others whose patriotism is, as Grant said, measured by dollars and cents; they will stoop to bribery and other questionable acts necessary to accomplish their object—the enrichment of themselves by defrauding the government or the public — and will try to use honest and honorable men in or out of office. It is sad to see so little conscience in some persons who claim to be patriots and gentlemen!

The general's relatives were frequently besieged by office-seekers to use their influence with him to secure positions for them of some sort or another. So long as he was President I received letters of application (during my residence abroad) with almost every American mail from office-seekers in nearly every part of the country, so much so that I suggested to him to let it be known that recommendations from his relatives had no weight with him; and that applicants for office must be recommended by the senators and congressmen of their respective States, or other well-known and responsible parties. On one occasion a young lady, whose parents had died and left her no means of support (her father was killed on the battlefield as an officer), requested me by letter to intercede with the President to give her a clerkship in the Treasury Department. I wrote to her that the President had nothing to do with the appointment of clerks in the different departments; that she must apply to the senators or congressmen of her State, etc.; that therefore I could not comply with her request, for it would do no good, however much I would like to see her appointed. Without securing the influence of these lawmakers she went to Washington, called on the President, and gave him my letter to read. The young lady informed me afterward that the President had said to her that he was pleased with the advice I had given her, and especially that

I didn't bother him with her application, and that for that very reason he took pity on her and procured for her the desired appointment.

Another instance showing the general's kind-heartedness toward and sympathy with suffering families is the following:

A boy eighteen years old, the only son of a royal officer of high rank in Leipzig, Germany, had committed a youthful indiscretion, and, fearing punishment, emigrated to New York. Being unable to secure employment he enlisted in the United States Army. Not being accustomed to the rough life of a soldier at the frontier he became ill. In his distress he wrote to his parents, confessing his wrongdoing, asking their pardon, and requesting them to get his government to intercede in behalf of his discharge. His father and mother came to my office (I was then United States consul in that city), and with tears in their eyes laid the case before me, asking me at the same time to plead with the President to discharge their only son. I did so, and with return mail I received copies of the discharge papers from the War Department. The boy returned home a reformed young man, and has since become a distinguished official. Happier parents and a happier son I never saw.

Another case is equally illustrative of the general's sympathy with suffering humanity:

A highly respectable family in Copenhagen, consisting of father, mother, and eight children (of whom the eldest was a boy eighteen years old), lost the husband and father by death. Up to that time they had nothing for their support but his small salary of six hundred dollars. With his death that income ceased. The boy had been preparing himself for a university course; but now he had to give up his studies and work for the support of his invalid mother and her seven small children.

It was difficult for him to get a position in which he could earn more than two dollars a week—an insufficient amount for their support.

A position in a New York business house was offered to him, with an income of eight hundred dollars. He came to this country, but only to find that the firm had failed. Here he was—penniless. What should he do? Finding no employment he enlisted in the United States Army; but his monthly pay, which he regularly sent to his mother, was insufficient to support the family. A little sister of his came to me of her own prompting (I was then United States Minister Resident in Copenhagen), stated the case of her mother and brother, and asked me with tears if I could not get him out of the army and into a business by which he could support the family. I promised that I would try. I laid the case before the President in almost the same words (in a translated form) used by the little girl, whose name was Ingeborg. In due time I was informed that the President had ordered the discharge of Ingeborg's brother, and had secured for him a position with a salary of a thousand dollars. Of course there was great joy in that household. The affectionate son and brother made remittances to his mother of fifty dollars every month. That same Ingeborg helped her mother, educated herself at my advice, learned some English, and finally married a well-to-do official. Inviting me to the wedding, she wrote in English, literally, as follows:

"I am hope that I should marry in Copenhagen at the entrance of August; you are indubitably entitled to be invited; we adjoin our portrats and send them you. My loved and I hope you will kondisdaen to go to our marriage. My mother send humeliat respect, and also I adjoin my venerable humbelness. INGEBORG L."

This is somewhat similar to the remark of another Danish young lady, who desired to emigrate to this country, "I to love America, I enemy Denmark;" or of a German woman referring to chickens, saying, "They are a strange people, I mean a curious folk;" or of a young foreigner learning our language, saying, "I walked into English."

CHAPTER XV.

Domestic Life.

THE following extracts from two letters addressed by the general, one to his sister in Copenhagen, and one to his father, give glimpses of his domestic life and of what he thought of his children. A part of the first letter refers to his "summering" at Long Branch, where a Mr. W., a friend of his sister, made an unsuccessful attempt to see him, not for the purpose of asking for an office, but of paying his respects to him.

The following is an extract from the first letter mentioned:

"WASHINGTON, D. C., October 26, 1871.

"MY DEAR SISTER: I have been intending to write you for some time; but the moment I get into my office in the morning it is overwhelmed with visitors, and continues so through the day. I now write of a rainy evening, after having read the New York papers.

"Jennie is with us, has been for some days, and will remain until she becomes homesick, which, I hope, will not be soon.

"I received your letter in which you gave me an extract from Mr. W.'s. I had no recollection or knowledge of the matter whatever. The fact is, I am followed wherever I go, at Long Branch as well as here. I sometimes shake off callers, not knowing their business, whom I would be delighted to see. In the case of Mr. W., however, I do not think that I ever knew that he had called. For the first time in my life I had arranged to go fishing at sea. To do so it was necessary to engage fishermen, with boat, beforehand. General P. did not know that I had made the arrangement, and probably was not at my house when I returned from riding, the evening after Mr. W. called. You will see the explanation. I will write it to Mr. W.

"Fred, after graduating at West Point, accepted a position as assistant civil engineer, and gave up a good portion of his furlough to go to work at his new profession. He has been in the Rocky Mountains since August, surveying, in pursuit of his new profession.

"But little or nothing can be done in the winter by him; I have, therefore, got him a leave of absence from his engineer duties to accompany General Sherman abroad until the latter part of April. I expect him to sail the next month. . . . I will instruct him to run up to Copenhagen from a convenient point and spend a few days with you. You will find him a well-grown and much-improved boy. He is about the height Brother Simpson was, and well developed physically. You will be pleased with him, I know.

"During the Harvard vacation, next year, I intend that Buck and Jesse shall go to Europe also. It may be that in the short time they will have to remain abroad they may not be able to go up to see you; but I think they will be pleased to do so, and may spare time for that purpose. I do not know but I owe an apology to Mr. Cramer for not answering his letters. All have been received, and I have been gratified with them. But I am so constantly pressed that it is almost impossible for me to get any time to devote to private correspondence.

"All send our kindest regards to Mr. Cramer, and love to you and the children. Yours affectionately,

"U. S. GRANT."

"P. S.—I shall always be delighted to receive letters from you and Mr. Cramer, whether I answer them or not."

The following is an extract from the President's letter to his father about his children, and will explain itself:

"EXECUTIVE MANSION, WASHINGTON,
June 2, 1872.

"DEAR FATHER: Hearing from home frequently as I do, through persons coming from there and through occasional letters, I scarcely ever think of writing. Hereafter, however, I will try to write oftener or have Jesse write. The children might all write to you, for that matter. We hear occasionally from Fred direct, and very often through the papers. He has enjoyed his European trip very much, and I think will be much improved by it. Nellie writes very often, and is a very much better letter-writer than either of the boys are. Her composition is easy and fluent, and she writes very correctly. She seems to have made a very good impression where she has been. Buck sails for Europe on July 6. He will travel but little, however. . . . His object is to acquire a speaking knowledge of both the French and German languages, both of which he is now quite a good scholar in.

"I received a letter from Mary a short time since. She said that she would leave for home about the first of June. You may expect her home by the twentieth, no doubt. Julia and Jesse are well, and send much love to you and mother.

"Sincerely yours, U. S. GRANT."

It is evident from the above extracts that the general was very much devoted to his children; that he carefully watched their progress in their growth, education, etc., and that he thought much of them, as well as of his relatives. A more devoted and affectionate husband, father, and friend than Grant can scarcely be conceived. He was always very careful of the feelings of others, and felt sorry when anyone who was not an office-seeker was disappointed in not seeing him after an effort had been made to that effect. There were few, if any, Presidents who carried on such an enormous private correspondence as he did. He seldom got his private secretaries to write any of his private letters.

The following letter, written to his aged and feeble father in response to one from the latter, expressing a desire to see him before the meeting of Congress, shows that, notwithstanding the pressure of official business in the form of reading the reports of the secretaries of the different departments and of preparing his own annual message to Congress, etc., he was willing and glad to please him at the sacrifice of his time and convenience:

"EXECUTIVE MANSION, WASHINGTON,
November 3, 1872.

"DEAR FATHER: I am in receipt of Mr. Brent's letter, dictated by you expressing a wish to see me, if possible, before the meeting of Congress. I think it will be possible for me to go this week, probably leaving here on Thursday or Friday next. I would like as far as possible to avoid meeting people while there. I hope, therefore, you will say nothing about my coming. Probably Julia, Fred, Nellie, and Jesse will accompany me. You probably have not room enough in the house for us all; but that will make no difference. Fred and Jesse can stay at the hotel. All are quite well. Yours truly,

"U. S. GRANT."

The following letter on the same subject shows the general's anxiety for his father's condition:

"EXECUTIVE MANSION, WASHINGTON,
May 31, 1873.

"DEAR SISTER: I am just in receipt of your letter speaking of father's rapid decline. Of course, I will go home at any day that it may be necessary for me to do so. I have been absent so much this spring that business has accumulated so that I cannot go very well just now, and next Thursday I have arranged to take us all to Long Branch. Any time after that I can go as well as not, and would not let that interfere if there should be a necessity. Don't fail to keep me advised of father's condition. Yours truly,

"U. S. GRANT."

Speaking one day of his parents the general said that his father was a remarkable man, naturally smart, with strong convictions, well read and intelligent, with a fine poetic mind; so much so that if he had had a superior education he would have become an excellent poet. Of his mother he said that she was the best woman he had ever known; unselfish, devoted to her family, thoroughly good, conscientious, intelligent, of a quiet and amiable disposition, never meddling with other persons' affairs, genuinely pious without any cant, with a strong sense of right and justice; unobtrusive, kind-hearted, and attached to her Church and country. I said, "General, you have most of your mother's characteristics;" to which he simply replied, "Yes, I think so."

Speaking of religion and devotion to the Church, he told me that on the occasion of a communion service being held in the Metropolitan Methodist Episcopal Church, in Washington, he requested Schuyler Colfax, who occupied a pew in front of the general's, to accompany him to the communion table, being anxious to partake of the holy communion; but he declined to go, "and so I, too, stayed away," the general said. This is an illustration of the influence of example. He thought that if professed Christians were more consistent in their practice the churches would be better attended and do more good. I told him that this was no excuse for not joining church, for counterfeit money presupposes genuine money, and so hypocrisy argues genuine piety. He admitted the truth of this statement, but said that people do not always think of it in that light.

CHAPTER XVI.

General Grant in Switzerland and France.

PERSONS who have traveled in Switzerland will read with interest the following letter from his pen in reply to one inviting him to visit us in Copenhagen:

"RAGATZ, SWITZERLAND, August 13, 1877.

"MY DEAR MR. CRAMER: Before leaving England I had accepted invitations to visit cities and country houses in Scotland—and places in England not yet visited by me—to take up all the month of September and part of October. I thought there was time for me to visit this interesting country and to make a run through Denmark, Sweden, and Norway, and get back to Scotland in time to keep my engagements. But I have found so much of interest here, and the modes of conveyance so slow in reaching the points of greatest interest, that it is already too late to even go to Denmark, leaving out Norway and Sweden. Already we have spent eight actual days in carriages in getting from point to point, exclusive of other modes of travel. We have visited most of the lakes and crossed the principal passes in Switzerland and northern Italy. It has all been exceedingly interesting to me, the greatest regret being that I had not more time. I intend yet to visit Denmark and the countries north of it; but whether this fall or next season is not yet determined; probably about next June.

"I am sorry not to be able to see Mary before she returns to America. I do not expect to return there before next July a year, and possibly not so early.

"All send love to Mary and the children, with kindest regards for yourself.

"Very truly yours, U. S. GRANT."

The following letter has a general interest. It was written in response to one from me concerning the case of a foreign diplomatist. It shows the willingness of General Grant to do justice to all parties, whatever their nationality or stations in life:

"PARIS, FRANCE, November 27, 1877.

"MY DEAR MR. CRAMER: I am just in receipt of your letter of the 21st instant, inclosing one from the Portuguese Minister —I suppose—to Denmark, recounting the cause of his brother-in-law's removal from the diplomatic service, etc. I knew Baron de S. and the baroness very well, and esteemed them very highly. There was never any difficulty with him in the State Department, or with any official in Washington, that I have any recollection of. I am very sure that no cause of complaint could have existed on our part without my knowing it. It would afford me the greatest pleasure to meet the baron and his wife during my European tour, but I fear I shall not be able to do so. My trip through Spain and Portugal has been put off, or at least postponed, for this year. On Saturday we leave here for the south of France, from there to take a naval vessel to visit all points of interest on the Mediterranean. We will probably go up the Nile, and put in the winter in a warm climate, to be ready for our northern tour in the spring. It is barely possible that when we return from our trip up the Nile we may go on east through China, Japan, etc., over to San Francisco. But this is not probable for another year. This will probably be the last opportunity I shall ever have of visiting Europe, and there is much to see that I have not seen, and cannot this winter.

"I hear from home occasionally, but not as often as probably you do. All were well by the last advices—received two days ago from Orville.

"Please assure your colleague that I have no recollection of other than the most pleasant relations between United States officials and the Baron de S.

"With kind regards from Mrs. Grant, Jesse, and myself, I am very truly yours,

"U. S. GRANT."

CHAPTER XVII.

In Egypt, Jerusalem, Ephesus, Constantinople, etc.

THE following letter has, to some extent, an historic interest, in that it, among other things, describes the condition of Constantinople at the time the Russian army besieged it:

"CONSTANTINOPLE, March 5, 1875.

"MY DEAR MR. CRAMER: On my arrival here I found your letter specially inquiring about the time I expect to be in Copenhagen. My plan is to be in Sweden by the middle of June, and after visiting that country and Norway to return by way of Copenhagen. It is not likely that I will be there before the fifth to the tenth of July; and it may be that I will like the northern country so well that my visit to

Copenhagen will be postponed even a month longer. We have had a delightful winter. Over a month was spent in Egypt, visiting the old ruins of that country under the most favorable circumstances.

"Leaving Cairo, we visited Suez and passed through the Suez Canal to Port Said. From the latter place we went to Joppa and out to Jerusalem. Since then we visited Ephesus and Smyrna, and are now here. The Russians are outside of the city, but do not come in. A stranger would not detect, from appearances, that an enemy was so near. In fact, I think the Turks now regard Russians as about the only people in Europe from whom they can expect anything.

"When you write home give my love to mother, Mary and the children, and Jennie.

"I will inform you later, when I know definitely, about the time to expect me in Copenhagen. Very truly yours,

"U. S. GRANT."

Referring, in our conversations at a later date, to the siege of Constantinople by the Russians, General Grant said that he never knew of a besieged place where so little of warlike preparations were seen as in that city at the time he was there. Concerning Abdul-Hamid II, Sultan of Turkey, with whom he dined, he said that he appeared to be a man familiar with the manners and customs of the European Christian nations, and not averse to them; that he seemed to be well versed in geography and military affairs; an intelligent and kind-hearted ruler who earnestly desired to promote the welfare of his people; but that he seemed to be in a state of unrest and apprehension, though he tried to conceal it all the time. The general thought that though the Sultan was not a bigoted Mohammedan he was, nevertheless, under the control of the Old Turkish party, which is opposed to every liberal or constitutional movement, as well as to all Christian influences, and that, therefore, the Christians of his empire could expect few, if any, favors at his hand. He thought it strange that though Russia began a war with Turkey and conquered it, "the Turks regarded the Russians as about the only people in Europe from whom they can expect anything." The reason of this he thought he saw in the autocratic form of government of both countries, both being determined to repress all liberal sentiments, even at the expense, if need be, of the Christian inhabitants of Turkey.* Personally, the general liked the sultan very much and was highly pleased with his interview with him.

Concerning his visit to Jerusalem he said that the impressions he received there were of a mixed character. Nowhere are

* This shows how correct General Grant's judgment was of the state of affairs in Turkey at the time he was there, and how clearly he foresaw the future action of that country in reference to the Christian inhabitants thereof.

the retarding effects of Mohammedanism upon the people more apparent, so far as he knew, than in that city. They are woefully behind the age there. How different is the present city from that described by David: "The perfection of beauty, the joy of the whole earth." And yet it is true of it to-day what is said of it in the Psalms: "Jerusalem is builded as a city that is compact together." He said he never felt so solemn in his life as he did in the presence of the places made memorable and sacred by the presence of Jesus Christ. While he had not studied the predictions of the Bible concerning Jerusalem and Palestine, yet, from what he had heard, read, and seen, he could not help noticing that some of them had been fulfilled.

CHAPTER XVIII.

More Letters from General Grant.

IT was not the intention of General Grant to keep me informed of all his movements, but only of those relating to his intended visit to Copenhagen, during which time my wife and children were in this country for the purpose of letting the latter attend school, that they might become, not "Europeanized," but "Americanized." This observation is made in explanation of the general's references, in several of his letters, to "Mary and the children."

"HOTEL LIVERPOOL, PARIS, May 25, 1878.

"MY DEAR MR. CRAMER: I am now for the first time able to fix, approximately, the time of my visit to Copenhagen. We will leave here on Saturday, three weeks from to-day, or on the following Tuesday. We will stop at The Hague three or four days. Jesse leaves for home so as to take the steamer on the 4th of June from Liverpool. Our party, therefore, will consist only of Mrs. Grant—with her maid—and myself. If your arrangements are made to be away from Copenhagen at the time mentioned above I beg that you will not change your plans. Should you be there we will probably remain over about one week. Should you be away we will stop only a couple of days.

"I have not heard directly from Elizabeth for some time: probably my own fault, for Mr. Corbin is very prompt in answering every letter. But Buckey writes regularly every week from New York, so I hear indirectly. When you write give my love to all of them at Elizabeth.

"Very truly yours, U. S. GRANT."

"P. S.—I go from Copenhagen directly to Stockholm. I am not personally acquainted with our present minister there, though I once appointed him to a South American mission. U. S. G."

"PARIS, FRANCE, June 3, 1878.

"MY DEAR MR. CRAMER: Your letter of the 31st of May is just received. I should have written to you within a day or two to inform you of a slight change of plan, which will bring me to Copenhagen from ten days to two weeks later than I wrote you I should be there, even if I had not received your letter. To save retracing my steps, as I should be obliged to do by the routes laid out in my last letter, I now intend to go from The Hague to Berlin, and visit a few German cities before going to Denmark. From Copenhagen I shall go by water to Norway, thence to Sweden, St. Petersburg, Moscow, and to Vienna.

"I shall be very glad indeed to see Mary and the children, and hope they may be back by the time I reach Copenhagen, about from the 5th to the 10th of July.

"Jesse sails from Liverpool to-morrow for home. He has been very homesick for some time.

"With best regards from Mrs. Grant and myself, I am very truly yours,

"U. S. GRANT."

"HANOVER, GERMANY, June 25, 1878.

"MY DEAR MR. CRAMER: Mrs. Grant and I are now here on our way to the German capital. We will probably remain in Berlin until Monday, the 1st of July. We will stop over by the way from Berlin to Copenhagen—particularly at Hamburg—so as to reach Copenhagen about July 5.

"If you will drop me a line to the Kaiserhof Hotel, in Berlin, to let me know if Mary will be home at the time designated, I will be obliged. If she is not to be at home I may change my plan and go direct to Sweden, thence to Norway, and return south to Denmark.

"Mrs. Grant and I are both well, and send much love to Mary and the children.

"Very truly yours,

"U. S. GRANT."

"BERLIN, GERMANY, June 29, 1878.

"MY DEAR MR. CRAMER: I have received your last letter, and am sorry to learn that Mary and the children will not be in Copenhagen at the time I propose being there. We will go on, however, as previously proposed, leaving here on Tuesday, the 3d of July, remain over the 4th, and possibly the 5th at Hamburg, reaching Copenhagen the same day. I will telegraph you from Hamburg the day and the hour of our departure and the line by which we will travel.

"Very truly yours,

"U. S. GRANT."

CHAPTER XIX.

Various Conversations with General Grant.

It was stated at the beginning that General and Mrs. Grant arrived in Copenhagen on the morning of the 6th of July, 1878, and remained there as my guests until the 12th of the same month, when they left by steamer for Christiania, Norway. During these six days we discussed many subjects, the leading thoughts of which I entered in my diary, which are here reproduced in their outline. Among the topics of our conversation was

PRINCE BISMARCK.

Omitting my own remarks I give here the substance of the general's observations. He said that he had spent several very interesting hours with Prince Bismarck, whom he considered one of the most charming and instructive conversationalists he had ever met with, overflowing with humor and wit, and throwing light on every subject he discussed. "Putting company at their ease, Bismarck entertains and amuses them for hours as few are able to do. Sometimes in a few words he draws the character of a prominent man or woman or a nation so correctly that it is really surprising, or he gives the gist of an event in a single sentence. He has a magnificent physique, and seems to be born to his high position. He is no doubt the greatest statesman of the present time. He knows how to make events and persons subserve his purpose. He loves to talk, and is courteous and kind to everyone in his presence. There are always 'points' in his conversation, and he knows how to draw out from men what he wants to know from them. His brief descriptions of men and nations are as humorous as they are generally correct. He may sometimes be arbitrary in his measures and views, but he seems to be always sincere and have the good of the emperor and of the fatherland at heart. I noticed that he thought a great deal of the old emperor. Germany owes much to Bismarck, whatever may be said of his autocratic bearing. Like myself, he enjoys a good cigar, and there we met on a footing of equality."

Of the German people the general said that what he had thus far seen of them and their country pleased him greatly. Everywhere the soil was under good cultivation; the people seemed to be intelligent and thrifty, loving their beer, tobacco, and fatherland.

VIEWS OF AMERICAN NATIONALITY.

The feeling of American nationality was highly developed in General Grant. In conversing with him on home affairs I asked him if he believed that our country would remain united. He replied in substance that since the late civil war the feeling of nationality had become stronger than it had ever been before. Our people take now a greater pride in being "Americans" than in being "Virginians" or "New Yorkers," etc. Local government, he said, far from diminishing the feeling of nationality, rather strengthens it. The idea of self-government is intensely developed among our people. No monarchy could ever be established here. According to him the strong feeling of nationality embracing the whole country has a tendency to assimilate all the various elements of our people—race, languages, customs, etc.—under our common political institutions. There are now fewer elements of real danger in the United States arising from the solution of the problem of nationality than there are in any other great and growing people. State after State has been taken into the Union without having a population alien in race, language, manners, customs, education, etc. This has been a fortunate thing for us. Civil and religious liberty, local and self-government, and our excellent common-school system have contributed largely toward gradually absorbing the immigrants and making our people a homogeneous nation. Hence no section of our country is inhabited with a hostile people—a fortunate thing for us. Excepting a few anarchists and other discontented foreigners we have no hostile people to contend against, for the majority of the foreigners that land annually on our shores come here to work and improve their personal and domestic condition. They are generally peaceable, if not excited by anarchists and half-educated lazy fellows.

In speaking of the means for preserving the Union and perpetuating our institutions General Grant said that great care should be taken to extend our common-school system to every nook and corner of our vast country, and to bring that system to its highest perfection; to cultivate in the rising generation love of country or true patriotism, and instill in their minds the idea of the indissolubleness of the Union. They should be taught "not to love Cæsar less, but Rome more;" that is to say, while loving the home State, they should love the country more. Hard sectional feelings should give way to brotherly love for the whole American family. Now, that the cause of the late great strife is forever removed, the whole nation, as one great family, should cultivate genuine brotherly feelings and endeavor to perpetuate the union of the States, the principles of the Declaration of Independence, and constitutional liberty.

Another safeguard of our liberties the general saw in our Protestant Churches and Sunday schools. While we have no State religion—and this is as it should be—yet we are in reality a Christian nation which owes much to the teachings of the Bible through the Churches and Sunday schools. There can be no question, in his opinion, as to the fact that the various humanitarian institutions in the several States owe their existence indirectly to the teachings of Christianity. He was glad to notice that there was so much religious activity in our country; and if the Churches and Sunday schools continue to do their duty, the danger growing out of lawlessness, anarchy, and the secret machinations of a countryless enemy will be diminished and overcome. The permeation of our people with the principles of Christianity will aid them in absorbing the promiscuous crowds of European immigrants and assimilating them in the body politic. But, notwithstanding this, greater restrictions ought to be laid upon immigration. No paupers, no criminals, no cripples, and none who are unable to read and write, ought to be permitted to land on our shores; while the franchise should be extended only to those foreigners who have in reality been five years in this country and are able to read and write. As to the Chinese immigrants, that is a problem that needs still further careful consideration.

Another thought of the general's was that no portion of our people ought to be subject to the dictation of a foreign potentate so far as their civil relations to the State are concerned. It might lead to dangerous complications, as is seen in Germany and Austria-Hungary and elsewhere; or it might lead to the overthrow of our civil institutions and religious liberty. It behooves our people to be on their guard in this matter, and not to elect men to legislatures and Congress, and to other responsible positions, who, for some reason or other, are influenced by foreign dictation. In this particular matter, as in every other dangerous affair, the general thought that "Eternal vigilance is the price of liberty."

The State authorities, the general thought, should never make any appropriation for any sectarian school or institution. It would be unjust to the taxpayer as well as to those denominations that receive no such grant; nor should these authorities provide religious instruction for the children in our public schools, though he had no objections to the reading of a few verses from the New Testament and the saying of the Lord's Prayer at the beginning of school hours.

As to the relations of capital and labor, he thought the government should never interfere in them, except to protect both alike from violence. This problem will adjust itself if left to the parties concerned under this law of protection.

He thought it a wise provision that only native citizens are eligible to be elected President of the United States, though in all other respects he favored the equality of all citizens alike; while all citizens should recognize the indivisibility and supremacy of the sovereignty of the United States; and those citizens who acknowledge and act under any other (foreign) supreme power should be deprived of the rights and privileges of citizenship. On the other hand, our government should protect all its citizens alike, at home and abroad.

CHAPTER XX.

How President Grant Vetoed the So-called "Inflation Bill."

IN September, 1873, a financial panic swept over the country, causing many business failures and disturbing the money markets of the world. The Forty-third Congress of the United States, that convened in the following December, grappled with this subject. The refunding of the public debt and the movement for the resumption of specie payment were checked for a while. There were many well-meaning men in and out of Congress who advocated so-called "fiat-money" in the form of an unusually large issue of "greenbacks." Even President Grant, at the beginning of the session of that Congress, had almost come to the same conclusion; for in his annual message he said, among other things: "I do not believe that there is too much of it [greenback circulation] now for the dullest period of the year."

During the latter part of its session that Congress passed what was then called "the inflation bill," and urged the President to sign it.

But in the meantime he had studied the question more carefully, especially that phase of it relating to our national credit abroad, and had arrived at a more conservative conclusion. Residing in Copenhagen at that time, I studied public opinion in Europe on that subject as expressed by the leading journals of England, Germany, and France, as well as by my colleagues in private conversations, and knowing that my letters to him on any subject were always welcome I wrote him privately a strong letter, stating what I had thus learned, namely, that that bill, if it became law, would strike a blow at our national credit in Europe, from the effects of which our country would not recover for a long time. The financial world in Europe was then on tiptoe to learn whether the President would sign or veto that bill.

Well, he did veto it, notwithstanding many Republican senators, and representatives for several days urged upon him the necessity of signing it. By that act, I told him, he rendered our country a service that, in my judgment, was, in importance, second to none of the battles he had won during the war.

He said that he never had any reason to regret having vetoed that bill, and then briefly described how he had prepared his veto message. I give it here substantially as he told it.

The first evening after the bill had been brought to him, and after the callers had left the White House, he read it over very carefully, and then sat down at his desk and wrote out all the reasons he could think of in favor of his signing it. Laying his manuscript in a drawer he retired for the night.

The following evening, after having carefully listened to all the arguments that senators and congressmen had urged upon him in the course of the day and evening in favor of the bill, he sat down to write out all the arguments he could muster against it, and, laying it beside the first manuscript, he retired for the night.

On the third evening he carefully read over both documents, reflecting for a while on the relative strength or weight of their respective arguments.

On the following morning he had come to the conclusion that, in order to avert a still greater financial calamity in the near future, the requirements of the existing situation, as well as the honor of the nation, demanded of him to veto the bill, and he caused his second document to be copied and the necessary formulas to be added, and, having thus prepared his celebrated veto message against signing the "inflation bill," he sent it to the Forty-third Congress.

It required a great deal of moral courage to veto that bill, passed as it had been by a Republican Congress. He told me that for several days he was uncertain what to do in the matter, for men in whose wisdom, statesmanship, and patriotism he had the fullest confidence, urged upon him the necessity of signing it; while, on the other hand, there were other men, equally wise and patriotic, who strongly advised him to veto it, pointing out the disastrous consequences that would follow from the bill becoming a law. But he took into consideration the necessity of maintaining the financial integrity of our country in the presence of the financial world of Europe. He told me that my letter on the subject, above referred to, influenced his mind in the right direction, because I had studied the question from the European point of view.

Whatever may be said to the contrary, Grant was extremely conscientious, and carefully studied every question laid before him for decision or action. His sole desire was to serve the whole country conscientiously and to the best of his ability. He told me that often during the sessions of Congress, after a day's hard work, and after having met the claims of society in the evening, he sat up till long after midnight to study the various cases and questions that had been submitted to him for action. He fully felt the tremendous responsibility of his office.

I asked him if he ever prayed for wisdom and guidance. He replied, "Yes, I often prayed silently to God at night and during the day that he might aid me in the performance of my duties, though I said nothing to anyone about it. I believe in the necessity of prayer, though I don't want to boast about it."

CHAPTER XXI.

Grant's Views About English Rule in India—Importance of Christian Missions.

THE following letter, addressed to me while still residing in Copenhagen, will be read with interest, as it clearly expresses Grant's views about English rule in India, as also his own and his wife's views of the work done by missionaries, especially in the educational line :

"RANGOON, BURMA, March 20, 1879.

"MY DEAR MR. CRAMER: We have now been very well through India, and are this far on our way to the farther East. The weather has been pleasant until within the last few days. But now it is becoming very warm, and as we have yet to go through the Straits of Malacca, near the equator, before turning north, we must expect some discomfort.

"I have been very much pleased with English rule and English hospitality in India. With that rule two hundred and fifty million of uncivilized people are living at peace with each other, and are not only drawing their subsistence from the soil, but are exporting a large excess over imports from it.

"It would be a sad day for the people of India and for the commerce of the world if the English should withdraw.

"We hope to be in Hong Kong by the middle of April, and farther north in China as soon thereafter as possible. When a good climate is reached we will regulate our further movements by the reports of weather on seas to be traversed and climate of places to be visited. At present, however, we expect to reach San Francisco about the first half of July. Although homesick to be settled down, I dread getting back. The clamor of the partisan and so-called independent press will be such as to make life there unpleasant for a time.

"Mrs. Grant joins me in love to you, Mary, and the children.

"I have to-day written a letter to Mr. Corbin. "Very truly yours,

"U. S. GRANT."

"P. S.—Julia asks me to add, and to tell Mary, that the English speak in the highest terms of the work being done all through this country by the missionaries, especially in an educational way. They say they are doing much good."

"U. S. G."

During a visit my wife and myself made at General Grant's home, No. 3 Sixty-sixth Street, New York city, from February 2 to February 9, 1882, I took occasion to make further inquiries of the general relative to the subjects touched upon in the above letter. Referring to English rule in India, he said, "that if it were not for the fact that the English government was ruling that vast country India would still be benighted and downtrodden." While he did not approve all that that government had done in that country, yet it owed to England the high degree of Christian civilization everywhere apparent there. "Agriculture, industry, commerce, education, railroads, etc., introduced and improved by the English, have started that country on a career of prosperity without which it would not even be as far advanced as the Chinese are. It is, after all, Christian civilization that raises the people of pagan countries in the scale of intelligent beings." I asked him if he did not believe Christianity to be the prime factor in our modern Christian civilization? He replied, "Certainly I do; and it is to be hoped that the Eastern nations will come to see it and adopt its fundamental principles." I further asked him if, judging from what he had seen and heard in these Eastern countries concerning Christian missions, he believed it to be justifiable in the different missionary societies of Christian countries to spend annually as much money as they do in the prosecution and maintenance of missionary work in the countries referred to? He replied: "Most certainly I do. If the missionaries, in connection with preaching, endeavor to educate the people, especially the rising generation, and cause them to be taught the Western arts of peace, that is, to improve their methods of carrying on agriculture and manufacture, as well as their modes of transportation; if they establish schools for all classes alike, and try to raise woman from her degraded position, the ultimate effects will be worth infinitely more than all the money the Churches may have expended on these enterprises. It is to be hoped that these missionaries will be sustained at home and in the countries in which they labor. They deserve it, for they do a noble and a good work."

Referring again to India, he said that it is one of the most remarkable facts in history that fifty or sixty thousand Englishmen, to say nothing of other Europeans and some Americans, manage a population in India of about two hundred and fifty millions, keep them in peace, and gradually teach them the Western civilization. It shows the superiority of the Christian religion over the pagan religions; "for," he further said, "there can be no doubt that religion, whatever its form may be, greatly influences the private and public life of a people and advances or retards their improvement in what we call civilization."

In reference to China he said that its people are very conservative and shrewd, disinclined to accept anything of our Western civilization, and hence far behind in what makes a nation truly great and strong. "I was treated very kindly while there," he said, "and they listened attentively to what I had to say to them. In some things they followed my advice, and I think it was for their advantage." The general thought that the commerce between the United States and China is not sufficiently developed; that the English are ahead of us; that we should send consuls there well qualified for the task of studying the best methods of extending the commerce between the two countries, and report the results of their investigations and the suggestions they have to make to our government; while the latter should encourage our merchants and manufacturers to seek a market for their respective goods in that country by concluding with it the necessary treaties to facilitate and protect the commerce and the life and property of all engaged in it. We should give the Chinese to understand that we do not come for conquest or to take undue advantage of them, but simply to extend the commerce between the two countries, and thus to establish friendly relations between them. The Chinese are shy of foreigners; they have some reason for it; but we should give them to understand that we seek nothing more than friendly commercial relations, in which both parties have an equal chance.

Concerning Japan the general said that he was greatly astonished at the progress they had made up to the time he was there. No Eastern country had pleased him so much as Japan. Its government had introduced many things of our Western civilization both in the army and navy and in civil life. He was highly pleased with her school system, especially with her technical schools, and with the fact that the English language is taught in them. He considered the emperor one of the most intelligent and progressive rulers of our time in the East, while the people, too, have made wonderful progress, considering that they are orientals. On my asking the general about the report of his having acted as the mediator between China and Japan in a certain important question pending at that time between the two governments, he smilingly said that he would rather not talk about himself, though it was true that he did effect a compromise, and thus averted a war, at least for some years. He did not approve the manner in which some of the European governments treat Japan. He advised the latter to enter into closer commercial relations with the United States, as Japan had nothing to fear from us except a fair commercial rivalry,

CHAPTER XXII.

Grant's Desire to Please his Friends and Relatives.

THE following " Letter of Introduction " shows General Grant's willingness to please his friends, and to aid them in " having a good time : "

" NEW YORK CITY, May 4, 1883.

" MY DEAR MR. CRAMER : This letter will present the Hon. Charles H. A. and family, friends of mine and neighbors in this city. Mr. A. goes abroad to see the Old World, and will probably remain there for a year or more. No doubt his summer travel will carry him into Switzerland, where I hope you may meet him.

" Mr. A. has been a personal as well as political friend of mine, and I hope you will be able to make his and his family's visit to the Swiss capital pleasant.

"Very truly yours, U. S. GRANT."

The following extracts from two letters —the one addressed to his sister, Mrs. Corbin, and the other to his niece, Miss Clara V. Cramer—show his solicitude for his relatives who, at the time the financial disaster overtook him, were residing in Berne, Switzerland. When the first letter was written the extent of that disaster was not yet fully known:

"NEW YORK CITY, May 8, 1884.

"DEAR JENNIE: I presume Fred has written to you—or will write—of the great disaster to the firm of Grant & Ward. He and I will endeavor to keep you from harm. . . . We are all well, and are trying to be happy. Do not be the slightest uneasy.

"Give our love to Mr. and Mrs. Cramer and dear Clara. Yours affectionately,

"U. S. GRANT."

"No. 3 East Sixty-sixth Street,
New York City, June 10, 1884.

"Dear Clara: Your letter, with one from your Aunt Jennie, reached me a few days since. I regret that I have not more cheerful news to write you than I have. Financially the Grant family is ruined for the present, and by the most stupendous frauds ever perpetrated. But your Aunt Jennie must not fret over it. . . . Fred is young and active, honest and intelligent, and will work with a vim to recuperate his losses. Of course, his first effort will be to repay his aunts. We go to Long Branch this week. We expected to live with Fred this summer in Morristown, N. J. But failing to rent our cottage we will occupy it, and Fred will live with us and rent his, if he can.

"All send love to you, your father and mother and Aunt Jennie.

"Yours affectionately,

"U. S. Grant."

Grant's integrity and moral heroism never shone more brilliantly than during and subsequent to the terrible financial disaster above referred to. Conscious of his rectitude, integrity, and honesty, he felt all the more keenly the insinuations, etc., that were for a short time thrown out against him by malicious parties. The heroic fortitude and silence with which he carried himself under those terribly trying ordeals were truly sublime, and, together with the magnificent patience he displayed during his long illness and approaching death, stamped him one of the world's greatest moral heroes. Right, justice, and virtue will always triumph in the end.

CHAPTER XXIII.

Grant Engaged in Writing his Memoirs.

THE following extract is from one of General Grant's last letters written before his death. It is addressed to his sister, Mrs. Cramer, who was residing at that date in Berne, Switzerland:

"NEW YORK CITY, January 13, 1885.

"DEAR SISTER: I am just in receipt of Jennie's letter of the 2d of January. I am busy on my book, which Fred is copying for the press. I hope to have it ready for the press by May next. But I may fail in this on account of weakness.

"My mouth has been very sore, but not so bad, I think, as some of the newspapers have made out. But it has been bad enough. The balance of the family are all well.

"I presume Jennie will be away before this reaches you. . . . All send love.

"Yours affectionately,

"U. S. GRANT."

CHAPTER XXIV.

Grant as a Man and Friend.

GENERAL GRANT was ever careful of the feelings of others, whether they were his friends or not. He never, consciously or willingly, hurt the feelings of anybody. He never spoke derogatively of anybody. If he expressed his opinion of any person that was not flattering to that person it contained nothing but his honest judgment expressed in a spirit of kindness.

He never used profane language. He told me that the nearest approach he made to swearing was the use of the word "confounded." Nor did he ever tell "smutty" anecdotes or allow others to tell such in his presence. At a certain summer resort he happened to be in a company of men one of whom was about to tell such a story, and, looking around, asked, "Are there any ladies here?" The general replied, "No, but there are gentlemen here." That man did not relate his anecdote.

He had a quiet way of getting rid of obtrusive persons. At that same place he was one morning about to take a walk in the woods, when a lady emerged from a company of her female friends and accosted him thus: "General, we are also about to take a walk; would you be willing to accompany us?" He simply replied, "Madame, you are very kind; but you must excuse me, I have made my arrangements for a morning walk."

He never used improper or coarse language anywhere, nor related stories that could not be told in the circle of the most refined ladies. He turned away with disgust from all coarseness and vulgarity. He was approachable to the humblest as well as to children. He was fond of the latter, because they were pure and innocent. He was very charitable, and aided financially many a poor person or family, and that in a very quiet and unobtrusive way. Indeed, when informed that such and such people were worthy of help, he was very liberal in his donations; and it made no difference of what nationality they may have been; but he was especially liberal toward the widows and orphans of soldiers and sailors. In our walks in Copenhagen he frequently handed a dollar, unsolicited, to women that had the appearance of being "honestly poor."

It is well known that he was a great smoker. He was very liberal with his cigars; for whenever he took one from his pocket to light it he generally offered one to every gentleman who happened to be present at the time. On one occasion, when my wife and myself were his guests, he offered me a cigar in her presence. She, remonstrating, said to him, "Ulys., don't lead my husband into temptation; for I married him as a non-smoking man." To which the general replied, in an amused way, "Mary, let Mr. Cramer smoke if he wants to; if he don't do anything worse he will get to heaven anyway." It is only proper to say here that he did not insist upon my smoking. He respected every person's conscientious convictions; nor did he endeavor to persuade them differently so long as they violated no human or divine law or the rules of propriety. He never "put on airs" either of superiority or "smartness."

If anyone showed him any favor he was sure to repay it in some form or other, if it was possible. He did not like to receive presents of any kind, and yet he disliked to disappoint by a refusal those who had the kindness to think of him in that way. Attentions of this character oppressed him. Nevertheless, he was always sincerely grateful for the kindness of the people, in whatever form it was manifested, as well as for their good opinion of him. He was averse to "fuss and feathers," or to pomp and show of any kind. He did not want anyone to go to any expense or trouble on his account. While in Copenhagen he would not permit me to give a banquet in his honor; and the one offered him by the Minister of Foreign Affairs he gratefully declined, saying that he "came to Copenhagen, not be feasted, but to rest." He appreciated good sermons and good speeches. He was present at the graduation of his niece, Miss Clara V. Cramer. She read the "essay of honor;" her subject was, "Our Indebtedness to Greece and Rome." He was so highly pleased with her performance that he gave her a hundred dollars in gold, and said, "That essay would have been a credit to a graduate of Yale or Harvard College."

CHAPTER XXV.

General Grant's Capture of Fort Donelson—His Virtual Arrest Subsequent to that Event—His Behavior in the Field.

IN his *Memoirs* General Grant refers to the capture of Fort Donelson, and to his virtual arrest after that event; but with characteristic modesty he refrains from giving all the details, or all the reasons leading up to this unpleasant occurrence. Some daily newspapers made unkind criticisms on the general concerning the so-called "complaints" or "charges" that had been preferred against him. It was natural that his father, then residing in Covington, Ky., opposite Cincinnati, should feel greatly concerned about the matter; so he wrote a letter to an officer of General Grant's staff, in whose veracity and frankness he had the utmost confidence, requesting him to give him a true account of the whole matter. He did so, signing himself only with the letter "H.," and sent also a copy of a letter written by General Halleck to General Thomas, of the War Department, in reference to said complaints.

These documents I found among Father Grant's papers. Though they were written with the permission to publish them, I do not know that they have ever been published (excepting General Halleck's letter). They throw fresh light on that episode, as well as on General Grant's private character, refuting in the most positive manner the "charges" both of his "profanity" and his "drink habits." It is to be remembered that this staff officer had up to that time always been with General Grant, and had thus had opportunities for observing the general in his daily walk and conversation; also, that he was a man of veracity, who enjoyed the confidence of Father Grant to the fullest extent, and who, if his statements relative to these "complaints" and "charges" had been false, might have gotten himself into trouble both with the authorities in Washington and with the public in general.

These letters or documents are given here in exactly the same form and words in which they were written:

"Jesse R. Grant, of Covington, Ky., the father of General Grant, being concerned to know the truth in relation to the complaints against his son, and his reported suspension from command after the capture of Fort Donelson, wrote a letter to a member of the general's staff, in whose veracity and frankness he had the utmost confidence, and has received the following letter of explanation, which he submits for publication:

"'PITTSBURG LANDING, April, 1862.

"'DEAR SIR: The inquiry as to the conduct of General Grant, ordered by the War Department, was solely with reference to matters subsequent to the capture of Fort Donelson. I send you herewith copies of correspondence between Adjutant General Thomas and General Halleck, which covers the whole ground of complaint, and pretty fully explains itself. It was Thomas's letter that was the foundation of the telegraphic dispatch to the Cincinnati papers, that the 'War Department had ordered General Grant to be superseded for bad conduct at Fort Donelson and elsewhere.'

"'In further explanation I would state that immediately after the surrender of Fort Donelson, General Grant issued the most stringent orders with reference to the captured property. He had several officers arrested for their violation, one of whom was the Provost Marshal of Clarksville. He did everything that a commander of an army to some extent demoralized by victory could do to enforce his orders. He had one regiment detailed solely for that duty. But in spite of all, so vast was the amount of plunder, and so great the eagerness of the soldiers and citizens to procure trophies, that even officers of high rank were willing to risk their commissions in their violation; and in spite of all precautions much of the captured property was surreptitiously carried off. So much for that complaint.'

"It will be observed that in the foregoing letter the exact date is not given, though it was written in April, 1862, from Pittsburg Landing.

"The following letter was also written from near Pittsburg Landing, and dated April 25, 1862; its contents indicate that it was written some days later than the preceding one. It is full of interest, and reads as follows:

"'IN FIELD, NEAR PITTSBURG LANDING,
TENN., April 25, 1862.

"'MY DEAR FRIEND: Here we are, advanced toward Corinth. Rain, rain, rain, is the daily chronicle of the camps. Talk about Potomac mud! It is not to be compared to the Tennessee mud. That awful road over which our brave troops marched from Fort Henry to Fort Donelson, when General Grant marched to accomplish that victory which was the death-blow to the rebellion, is the only one comparable to the road to Corinth. With twenty-eight thousand troops he not only took that stronghold, but at the same time took Bowling Green and Nashville, which one hundred thousand troops, under the generalship of the brave Buell, had failed to accomplish.

" ' " Did Buell cooperate in the taking of Fort Donelson ? " Let us see. But first let me remind you of Grant's celebrated | I should rather say notorious—" expedition against Columbus," where twenty-five (?) thousand men " marched up the lane, and then marched down again." You remember it well. Grant's friends had high hopes at the promise and great disappointment at the result. That expedition was made to divert the enemy and enable Buell to attack Bowling Green, which he failed to do. How was it reciprocated? You remember an order of General Halleck's, in which he thanked Major General Hunter for his aid and cooperation in the capture of Fort Donelson. It meant to thank Hunter; but it meant much more. You will appreciate that order better when I narrate a few facts which have come into my possession.

"'When Grant, with an army of less than twenty thousand men, was about to march on Fort Donelson, General Halleck telegraphed to General Buell: "Grant is about to attack Fort Donelson. Can't you send him reinforcements?" Buell's answer was, "I have none to spare." Soon after Halleck telegraphed: "The enemy are evacuating Bowling Green and reinforcing Fort Donelson. Can't you attack

Bowling Green?" Buell answered, "I am not prepared." Halleck then telegraphed, "Can't you make a demonstration?" Buell replied, "I never make demonstrations." And so Grant was left with twenty-eight thousand troops and the gunboats to strike the blow which drove the rebel army from Kentucky and Tennessee and from their stronghold at Manassas.

"'What has been his reward? The *Cincinnati Gazette*, a paper making great pretensions to high-toned morality and impartiality, uses such language as this concerning him: "But even in case of victory time should be taken to receive the full reports and find out who it was that attacked, pursued, and captured the enemy and took intrenchments at the point of the bayonet, and who were tardy and inert while the battle was going on. By a proper exercise of this moderation the government might avoid the extraordinary predicament of promoting a commander to a major generalship one day and suspending him from command the next, and eventually restoring him, chiefly to save its own consistency." No baser paragraph was ever published in the most venal press on earth. There is not a line in it that is not pregnant with most malicious falsehood. The editor of that paper either deliberately stated as a fact what he knew to be false, or he stated as a fact something concerning the truth or falsity of which he was ignorant. In either case he has committed a grave crime.

"'It is enough to assure you that every act and order of General Grant, in the investment and capture of Fort Donelson, met with the cordial indorsement and freely expressed approbation of the commanding general of the department. True, he was absent in the necessary discharge of duty at the gunboats at the time of the terrible conflict between McClernand's division and the enemy on our right on

Saturday morning. But he had so disposed his forces as to enable McClernand, as he eventually did, to check and repulse the advance of the enemy there, and had sent a portion of his staff, with authority and instructions to represent him; while the brilliant and successful charges of General C. F. Smith on our left and Colonel Morgan L. Smith on our right, on Saturday afternoon, were made by the order and under the immediate supervision of General Grant in person.

"'I shall not soon forget the reply of General Smith to a remark by General Buckner, on the morning of the surrender. It indicated the soldier and the gentleman. Immediately after General Smith came in and was saluted by General Buckner the latter remarked, "You made a brilliant charge and terribly surprised us on our right yesterday afternoon, General Smith. It decided the day against us." "I simply obeyed orders, nothing more, sir," was General Smith's prompt reply.

"'No complaint whatever was ever made by the President, or the War Department, or any other authority, or any responsible man, for any action or want of action on the part of General Grant in the investment and capture of Fort Donelson. He has received no allusion to it by any authority above him, except unqualified praise. I speak what I know. * *.'"

[Extract from a letter written by a friend in the army in Tennessee to a friend and relative of General Grant's in this vicinity.

The following copy of a letter from General Halleck explains itself:]

"The following is a copy of General Halleck's letter to General Thomas, alluded to in the above. It relates to 'complaints' against General Grant at that time:

"'HEADQUARTERS DEP'T OF THE MISSISSIPPI,
SAINT LOUIS, March 15, 1862.

"'*Brigadier General L. Thomas, Adjutant General of the Army, Washington:*

"'GENERAL: In accordance with your instructions of the 10th instant I report that General Grant and several officers of high rank in his command, immediately after the battle of Fort Donelson, went to Nashville without my authority or knowledge.

"'I am satisfied, however, from investigation, that General Grant did this from good intentions, and from a desire to subserve the public interests. Not having advice of General Buell's movements, and learning that General B. had ordered Smith's division of his [Grant's] command to Nashville, he deemed it his duty to go there in person. During the absence of General Grant and a part of his general officers numerous irregularities are said to have occurred at Fort Donelson. These were in violation of the orders issued by General

Grant before his departure, and probably under the circumstances were unavoidable.

"'General Grant has made the proper explanations, and has been directed to resume his command in the field. As he acted from a praiseworthy although mistaken zeal for the public service in going to Nashville and leaving his command, I respectfully recommend that no further notice be taken of it.

"'There never has been any want of military subordinations on the part of General Grant, and his failure to make returns of his forces has been explained as resulting partly from the failure of colonels of regiments to report to him on their arrival, and partly from an interruption of telegraphic communications. All these irregularities have now been remedied.

"'Very respectfully,

"'Your obedient servant,

"'(Signed,) H. W. HALLECK,

"'Major General.'

"Again, General Grant was complained of because he failed to make a return of his forces immediately after the battle. His failure to do this, and the commander of the Eastern forces not knowing within two or three thousand of the exact strength of Grant's army, 'disarranged the whole plan of operations on the Potomac!' Now, immediately after the battle, General Grant issued orders to division commanders to send as soon as possible reports of their commands. This was done without reference to the 'repeated orders from Washington and Saint Louis,' only one of which—owing to the cutting off of telegraphic communication—was ever received. But it was utterly impossible to get the division reports promptly. I need only cite one fact to prove this. The last report received was from General C. F. Smith—who is universally acknowledged to be one of the best disciplinarians in our army—and when Grant sent a report to Saint Louis, which was at the earliest practicable moment, he had to estimate General Smith's strength, his report not having been received up to that time. So much for this complaint.

"Now, as to his leaving his command and going to Nashville. The day after the capture of Fort Donelson General Grant received an order placing him in command of the 'District of West Tennessee.' The order gave no boundaries to the district other than the name would suggest, and the only natural boundary seemed to be the Cumberland River. If that were the true boundary, Nashville was in his district. He wrote to General Halleck that he would occupy with his forces Clarksville on Friday, and the succeeding Friday he would take possession of Nashville, unless he received different orders in the interim. Clarksville was occupied accordingly. In the meantime General Buell, with Mitchell's division of his army, moved on and halted his column nine miles from Nashville, and sent an order to General C. F. Smith to move his command, which was part of Grant's army, from Clarksville to Nashville. About the same time General Nelson came up the Cumberland with his command, ten thousand strong, with instructions from the Secretary of War to report to General Grant for duty. Grant not only permitted Smith to obey Buell's order, but sent Nelson, convoyed by a gunboat, on to Nashville. Grant knew very well that Nashville was already evacuated and white flags were floating over the city, and that the citizens were anxious for the approach of our army to take possession and protect them from the ravages of the rear guard of the rebel army. It was at this time, and under these circumstances, that Grant wrote to Halleck that unless some order was received by the next day directing his movements he would proceed to Nashville and have a conference with Buell as to his movements and the movements of the enemy. He went to Nashville, saw Buell, remained five or six hours, and returned to Fort Donelson. Nothing was ordered, and nothing transpired requiring his presence during his absence. These were General Grant's offenses, nothing more.

"These have been made the pretext for an amount of abuse and defamation which no other man in the army has received. The fact is, the army, as well as the civil walks of life, has many aspirants for preferment, and they seem to think that every man who has earned the favor of the people stands in their way and must be stricken down. You know as well as I that General Grant has no political aspirations. Often have I heard him express the wish that there was a law rendering every officer in the army unqualified for civil office for life. I know this further fact, that he has never sought, nor has any friend of his with his sanction, asked for his promotion in the army. Long ago, when he was commanding the District of Cairo, an influential friend of his, Mr. Washburne, wrote to him from Washington with reference to his promotion to a major generalship. General Grant promptly replied not to ask it—that no major generalships should be given until they were earned by actual services in the field.

"You know that when he left his business at Galena and went to Springfield with a company as their drillmaster, he did not ask or desire a position in the army. Day and night he worked at Springfield, doing all the drudgery of organizing the army of Illinois—drafting blanks, instructing quartermasters, mustering troops, making out reports, and doing everything that was asked by Governor Yates. While other men, especially those having military experience, were seeking the offices in the gift of the governor, Grant was patiently and unceasingly toiling with no object in view but the public good.

"It was at this time that, at the earnest solicitation of Governor Yates, he took command of a regiment whose disorganization and want of discipline had made it notorious. Yates insisted that Grant was the only man he knew that could manage it. He marched his regiment into Missouri, and made it a model regiment for discipline and effectiveness. I have heard it said that it was the only regiment quartered in Missouri against which no complaints were made for depredating.

"While Grant was quietly performing his duty with his regiment in the interior of Missouri, cut off almost entirely from communication with the rest of the world, he picked up a paper one morning and saw the announcement of his nomination and confirmation as brigadier general. Nothing could have more astonished him. He did not know that he had 'a friend at court,' and he had never thought or spoken of promotion. But there were men who had watched his progress in Missouri and knew his military capacity and untiring vigilance. Soon after he took command of the District of Cairo, and from that day to this his history is part of the history of the country. Whatever the papers may say by way of detraction, the general has thus far received the confidence and indorsement of his superiors.

"Anyone knowing him as you and I know him would suppose that, whatever might be said about his official conduct, no one would ever assail his private character. But this has been done. General John A. Logan was asked in Washington a few weeks ago, 'What kind of a man is Grant, I mean his private character?' 'Sir,' replied Logan, 'he is one of the very best men I ever knew.' This may have been an extravagant opinion, but it was an honest one, I have no doubt.

"Grant has been charged with drunkenness! No decent man can be found responsible for the report. I do not know a more abstemious man in the army. During that terrible siege of Donelson, when the elements seemed to have conspired to exhaust the strength of the besiegers, and some stimulant seemed absolutely necessary to health, he invariably refused to take one drop of liquor. It required a clear head as well as a strong arm to strike that fatal blow.

"There is another thing that can be said of the general that can be said of few men in the army. I do not believe any man ever heard him utter an oath. I have been with him under all manner of circumstances, and have seen him in anger, but never heard a profane word from him. If you knew the fearful amount of profanity there is in the army, and especially in the battlefield, you would appreciate the rareness of his virtue in this respect. The highest compliment I ever heard him pay his early instructors was a remark he made one day that he 'did not remember of ever having used an oath in his life.' For a man who is not a religious man to say that shows great reverence for the example and teachings of his childhood.

"Yours truly, H."

In whatever light we may view General Grant, he stands before the world a great man, great in his achievements, but still greater in his moral nature. His character as it really was has not yet been fully or correctly drawn. Prejudice, in some form or other, still lingers in some minds; nor have all excellent traits therein been fully brought out. His singleness and inflexibility of purpose, his conscientiousness, his devotion to duty, his sterling integrity, his true nobility, his refinement of nature, his kind-heartedness, his carefulness for the feelings of others, his pure and ardent patriotism, his strong sense of right and justice, his affectionate devotion to his family, the purity of his daily life, his strong common sense, his well-informed mind, his comprehensive intelligence, the quickness of his apprehension, his clear and far sightedness, his long-suffering under abuse and unjust criticism, his calmness amidst danger, his resignation amidst overwhelming misfortune, his heroic patience under a terrible and painful illness, his reverence for moral purity and goodness, his resolute determination for the triumph of truth and right, his trustfulness in the hour of sorrow, his undaunted courage on the battlefield, his endurance under severe trials and burdens, his serenity amid the stormy elements of passion, his composure amid strong temptations, his just views on religion and Providence, his ready recognition of merit in others, his silence under calumny, his unselfishness in the midst of self-seeking politicians and office-seekers—these qualities of his character stand out in solemn grandeur and tower far above the great mass of people; and we see in them a sight more truly noble than any mere warrior or conqueror the earth ever nursed on her bloody bosom, and one that in the eye of God is greater than any king or emperor that ever sat upon the throne of ambitious dominion.

How little do we know of his brain sweat, his heart labor, his conscience struggles, of his many days of toil, his many nights of weariness, his many months and years of vigilant, powerful effort, that were spent in achieving success and in perfecting what the world has bowed to in reverence! He was the son of perseverance, of unremitting toil and industry. He toiled long and hard, and his successes and greatness were due, not so much to his genius (if he had any), as to his perseverance and industry. Like many other successful men, he owed more to his unremitting toil, industry, and perseverance than to his native talents, or to his friends, or to favorable circumstances, or to all these combined. His work, whatever it was for the time being—he thought for it, planned for it, labored for it, lived for it. He never waited for favorable circumstances. Like Napoleon I, he made circumstances. He knew that he could not go to sleep and wake up an Alexander, a Napoleon, a Wellington, a Blucher. He knew that genius makes one great effort, then flutters, darts, and tires; but that hard work and perseverance wear and win; and he won by these qualities.

Reader, why do we hold up before us the example of great and good men? Because the use of these examples is to inspire others. The succession of all high and noble life is through personality. The fascination that draws us to the great and good is deep and divine; it is a call to share their greatness and goodness. If we get close to men of energy and see how they work, to men of strength and thought and see how they work, we will catch their spirit and method, and it will lift us into the atmosphere of purity and greatness and power, and energize and purify our whole being.

Grant was a noble and heroic example of devotion to duty, to liberty, and to country—a country that is freedom's cradle and liberty's home, religion's altar and humanity's shrine, learning's retreat and the arch of safety, and holding out the olive branch of peace. He endeavored to make strong our country's right arm of virtue and honor and safety, and to lay deep the principles of the permanence, prosperity, and glory of our republic. Let us all do likewise !

THE END.

www.ingramcontent.com/pod-product-compliance
Lightning Source LLC
LaVergne TN
LVHW011216110826
845150LV00006B/1445

* 9 7 8 1 4 2 5 5 1 7 1 6 8 *